Shelter Cats

Karen Commings

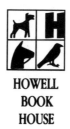

**HOWELL
BOOK
HOUSE**

New York

This book is dedicated to my four shelter cats, Peaches, Cary, Mocha and Maggie Mae, and to shelter cats everywhere who wait patiently for someone to adopt them.

Howell Book House
A Simon & Schuster Macmillan Company
1633 Broadway
New York, NY 10019-6785

Macmillan Publishing books may be purchased for business or sales promotional use. For information please write: Special Markets Department, Macmillan Publishing USA, 1633 Broadway, New York, NY 10019-6785.

Library of Congress Cataloging-in-Publication
Commings, Karen.
    Shelter cats / Karen Commings.
    p.   cm.
    Includes bibiographical references (p.   ).
    ISBN 0-87605-676-1
    1. Cats.   2. Cat adoption.   3. Animal shelters.   I. Title.
    SF447.C645   1998
    636.8   dc21   97-51968
                                                CIP

Manufactured in the United States of America
10 9 8 7 6 5 4 3 2 1

Book design by Scott Meola
Cover Design by Amy Trombat

Acknowledgments

My special thanks to Linda Parkin, Collection Development Librarian for the Dauphin County Library System, for suggesting that I write this book.

I would like to express my sincere appreciation and thanks to all of the people who contributed help and assistance, information and photographs to this book.

American Humane Association, Denver, CO: Doug Trowbridge, Program Coordinator for the Animal Protection Division.

American Veterinary Medical Association, Chicago, IL.

Animal Friends, Inc., Pittsburgh, PA: Lori Dalesio, Executive Director, and Margaret Stanley, volunteer and photographer.

Animal Welfare League of Alexandria, Alexandria, VA: Jeanine Larsen, Director of Humane Education.

Annette Carricato, D.V.M., Mountain View Animal Hospital, Harrisburg, PA.

Cat Fanciers' Association, Manasquan, NJ: Carol Krzanowski, Associate Director.

Denver Dumb Friends League, Denver, CO: Lani Kian, Communications Manager.

Four Footed Friends, Indiana, PA: Susan Steigman, President of the Board of Directors, and Linda Testa, volunteer.

Fried's Cat Shelter, Michigan City, IN: Lisa Szirovecz, Director of Public Relations.

Helen Opperman Krause Animal Foundation, Inc., Dillsburg, PA: Paula Shaner, President, and Eileen Wolfe, pet placement person.

Humane Society of Harrisburg Area, Inc., Harrisburg, PA: Edward M. Shore, Executive Director, and Linda Spangler, Development Coordinator.

Humane Society of the United States, Washington, DC: Mary Wilson and K. McCarthy, Companion Animals.

Alan Kirmayer, D.V.M., Animal Hospital of Rye, Marysville, PA.

Marin Humane Society, Novato, CA: Jolie Levine, Director of Public Relations, Darlene Blackman, SHARE Program Coordinator, and Elaine Sichel, photographer.

North Country Animal League, Morrisville, VT: Jan Gordon Stangel, Executive Director.

Pasadena Humane Society, Pasadena, CA: Steve McNall, Executive Director; Sandy DeMarco, Volunteer Coordinator, and Maggie the cat.

The Pet Authority, Harrisburg, PA: John Dunstan and Tom McGinley, owners, Rupert the cat.

The Pet Food Institute, Washington, DC.

Pet lovers: Melanie Bogardus, Steve and Tim Barker, and Essie Newman.

San Francisco Society for the Prevention of Cruelty to Animals, San Francisco, CA: Richard Avanzino, President, Paul Glassner, photographer and editor of Our Animals, and Lynn Spivak, Director of Public Relations.

Tree House Animal Foundation, Inc., Chicago, IL: Robin Dillow, Acting Director, and Sandra Newbury, Feline Socialization Specialist.

John C. Wright, Ph.D., Animal Behavior Society.

And the tens of thousands of shelter staff and volunteers across the United States who work tirelessly for the continued welfare and well-being of pets everywhere.

Contents

Foreword

Cats have not always enjoyed the best of times during their domestic history with human beings. Human history confirms how ethically inconsistent we can be as a species and how morality and sentiment can change like the whims of fashion. In various times and places, cats have been revered, demonized, and tortured for human amusement, education and "scientific" curiosity. Now cats are back in fashion as human companions, out-ranking dogs, at least numerically, in U.S. households. Yet even today, cats are often treated as mere objects. Many are discarded when they are no longer kittenish toys for children to play with. Others are abandoned because they are "too much trouble" for those people who have not made the necessary effort to understand cats' basic needs and behavior. Then there are those uninformed and uncaring people who allow their cats to roam free, to breed and to even go feral, becoming wild and unadoptable, along with their ever-multiplying offspring.

These are some of the reasons why animal shelters across the U.S. and in many other countries have so many dogs and cats and litters of offspring up for adoption. Thousands are still being destroyed every month.

The problem of homeless and abandoned cats should concern us all, not just cat lovers and humanitarians. Cats and other animals are part of the community where we live, be it rural, urban or suburban. To live in isolation from and in total disregard for the non-human members of our community, be they plants or animals, and be they wild or domestic, is all too easy and all too common.

The power of Shelter Cats is that it reminds us with great clarity what community really means by taking us into one of the most important but generally not widely recognized and supported components of any caring community: The animal shelter. Animal shelters filled with unwanted, lost and abused animals reflect a tragic breakdown in community.

It is a sad irony that some of the most caring and compassionate people work in animal shelters and it is they who have to take on the burden of an uncaring, indifferent, throw-away society, rehabilitating "disposable" pets, and often having to euthanize them. Not all shelters are "no-kill" because of the sheer volume of abandoned animals that come in every week. As the author Karen Commings suggests, you can volunteer in many ways at the animal shelter and help those non-human members of your community who are in need. Such service can be deeply rewarding, and the opportunity to help animals can be so personally gratifying for some adults and teenagers that a new career horizon of compassionate service may open up.

The more immediate rewards, however, of adopting one or more cats or kittens from your local animal shelter, and how to avoid various potential problems (like your resident cat not accepting a new cat or the new cat becoming a house-soiler) form the practical core of Karen's book.

In this heart's core, you will find sound advice on properly caring for your feline companions; why neutering is important; what common health and behavioral problems and emergencies you may face; what necessary preventive steps you need to take to avoid feline diseases, accidents, and injuries; and how to make indoor life safe and satisfying for cats.

The author breaks new ground in writing about how animal shelters operate and what community benefits they provide, including humane education for children and pet-facilitated human therapy. I am glad that she includes reference to the rights of cats, which helps us identify our personal and community responsibilities and duties toward cats and other animals.

The magic of this book is that it provides the reader with the necessary facts and insights to not only make the adoption of one or more felines from the local animal shelter a breeze—it also covers all the relevant areas of responsible and compassionate cat care for people who already have cats. Shelter Cats also presents a very convincing argument in favor of multiple cat households. This makes me feel less alone in my long-held view that it is probably inhumane just to keep one cat (or dog) alone in the home; and that cats do get on well together in properly managed groups, and are healthier and happier than those who live alone.

Dr. Michael W. Fox
Veterinarian and author of
Understanding Your Cat and other books

Introduction

In 1985, I adopted my first cat in more than seven years. The death of Snorkel in 1978 had left me so saddened that I couldn't deal with having another cat around the house until the hurt of losing him had healed. The opportunity to adopt Pokey, and save him from a certain death happened at a time in my life when I had a space that needed to be filled. As it turned out, Pokey was so endearing and lovable that I felt quite guilty about leaving him at home during the day while I was at work.

As a result, I headed to a no-kill animal shelter in downtown Pittsburgh to find Pokey a playmate just three months after I welcomed him into my home. Animal Friends, Inc., is a no-kill shelter which was and still is located in the heart of the Pittsburgh strip district where fresh fish and vegetables come into the city to be distributed to restaurants or sold at the strip's market locations.

I went to Animal Friends on a Friday evening thinking that if I found a suitable playmate for Pokey, I would have the whole weekend to acquaint them with each other (and the new cat with me), before going back to work Monday morning. Full of hope and high expectations, I carried Pokey's cat carrier with me to safely bring home a second cat should I find one.

At the shelter, I went from cage to cage talking to and petting the wonderful cats who were there. One of the cats particularly attracted me because she immediately began purring as soon as I started talking to her. It was the loudest purr I had ever heard. The card on her cage indicated her name was Peaches. Peaches. How sweet. She was a little tortoiseshell cat with white feet and a tan hourglass shape on her face that framed the area around her mouth and made it look petite and pretty. She was obviously interested in my voice as I approached her. When I opened her cage, she allowed me to pick her up and hold her during which time she continued non-stop her magnificent purr.

I would have walked out with Peaches in a heartbeat if finding a companion for me was my only consideration. But I had Pokey to think about and was concerned deeply about his relationship with a new animal in the house. Pokey was a sensitive and intensely affectionate cat. Because he had lived alone in a single-cat household for almost all of his short life, I had no idea how he would react to any cat I brought home. The last thing I wanted to do was to destroy his trust and gentleness by bringing in a cat who was in any way aggressive or dominant. After all, my house was Pokey's house, and it offered him the security to keep him feeling as though all was right with the world. I didn't want to upset the apple cart.

To help me make the decision about whether Peaches would be a good match, I observed the Animal Friends volunteers who were there playing with the cats, one of which was Peaches. Several of the cats had been taken out of their cages and were engaged in play activity in one of the shelter rooms. While the other cats jumped at a feather attached to a string or chased a ball across the floor, little Peaches sat quietly in one corner of the room watching what went on. She seemed reserved and unlikely to give Pokey a hard time.

When she was put back in her cage, I spent some more time with her, picking her up, holding her and listening to that extravagant purr that still lulls me to sleep at night. To help with the decision, I took a look at the shelter's intake forms to learn a little about Peaches' background. Her former owner had indicated that Peaches got along with people and other cats except that the owner's Siamese fought with her. So, instead of trying to solve the behavior problem that kept the Siamese and Peaches from getting along, the owner relinquished Peaches to Animal Friends, a solution that was a lot easier than working out the differences experienced between the two animals.

I also learned from the intake forms that Peaches had been vaccinated and spayed three months earlier, that she had no problem using her litter box and that she preferred dry food to canned. Hah! I thought. Given a choice, no cat would prefer dry food to canned.

Convinced that she would be a good fit in my household of one other cat, and determined to prove that, if canned cat food were offered to her, she would be an instant convert, I brought nine-month-old Peaches home that evening to thirteen-month-old Pokey, who apparently had not seen another cat since kittenhood. He followed around behind her for about three hours while she explored my house. In spite of the fact that my introduction of her to him was not even close to being proper and correct from a feline standpoint, it worked out for the best. Pokey and Peaches are still best friends. And to this day, Peaches still prefers dry food to the twice-daily feedings of canned. This was the first lesson she taught me.

Not everything was a bed of roses, however. In spite of the fact that, on the surface, Pokey accepted Peaches, his reaction toward me became somewhat distant for a while after I brought her home. He stopped sleeping on my bed at night and did not purr for more than two years. As he has grown older, his affection has returned and once again, I'm treated to the weight of Pokey's body draped over my legs as I sleep.

Within a month or so after bringing Peaches home, she developed a behavior problem. For some reason, she began to use Pokey's wicker bed as a litter box. I had her examined by a veterinarian to make sure that no health problem was causing the behavior anomaly. Satisfied that the activity was not medically motivated, I returned home wondering how to solve the problem.

Over the course of several days, I noticed that Peaches only used Pokey's bed as her litter box if I didn't get up, at her encouragement, to prepare their breakfast. The litter boxes were two flights down in the basement so Peaches might have been afraid she would miss something if she went all the way down there when what she really wanted was to be fed. The next morning, as soon as Peaches tried to awaken me, I got up and carried her down to the basement saying, "let's potty" to her and placed her in the litter box. I waited patiently for her while she did her business. After she was finished, I praised her, and the three of us, Peaches, Pokey, who by now had come to the basement to find out why I was down there instead of in the kitchen fixing breakfast, and I headed back upstairs to have our morning meal. That process continued for three days.

On the evening of the third day, when I opened the door from the garage to the basement after coming home from work, Pokey and Peaches were there as usual to greet me. As soon as Peaches saw me enter, she flew from the garage door across the cellar to the litter box and immediately urinated. Obviously, she wanted to let me know she knew it would please me. And it did. After praising her profusely, we three headed upstairs, this time for our dinner. Peaches has never urinated out of her litter box again, and I never stopped telling her, when she was in the litter box, what a great cat she was. It showed me what a little effort could do to modify a cat's behavior. That was the second in a long string of lessons that I learned from Peaches, a shelter cat rejected by her former owner and left to find another one willing to make her a permanent part of her life.

In addition to acquiring Peaches on that Friday night in September of 1985, I also acquired an interest in the activities that were going on at the shelter. *Volunteering my time petting and playing with cats?* That thought intrigued me. What else might I be able to do to for the benefit of these animals?

Shortly after I adopted Peaches, I contacted Animal Friends to offer my time in service to the shelter. It sounded more like fun than work. Through its experienced volunteers, the shelter offered some training to me and the others who had volunteered at the same time. We had our choice of activities, fund-raising, newsletter writing, dog washing, dog walking, cat socializing. *Cat socializing.* Hmmm. I had found my niche. So, in the fall of 1985, I began going to Animal Friends every Sunday afternoon to pet and play with the cats and help them become more accustomed to being handled by humans.

Of course, seeing so many wonderful cats at Animal Friends made me want to adopt even more. During the two years I spent there, I brought home a tuxedo named Cary and a shy white cat with piercing amber eyes, orange eyebrows and an orange striped tail named Spencer. The four cats had no trouble accepting each other, and three—Pokey, Peaches, and Cary—are still with me, Spencer having passed away in 1994. So good was my experience with these cats, that it inspired me to bring even more into my home, including Mocha, whom I obtained at the Humane Society of Harrisburg Area. Mocha forced me to adopt him when I visited the shelter one evening to pick up a ticket to a fund-raising event. He purred when I approached his cage in much the same way that Peaches did so many years ago at Animal Friends. When I opened Mocha's cage, he placed his paws on my shoulder and began rubbing my face. That was all it took to convince me to bring him home.

Mocha was taken to the shelter as a stray, but obviously had spent time with a human who cared for him. He was neutered and his front feet were declawed. Although none of my other cats are declawed, I was confident enough in their behavior to know that he would not feel threatened or be forced to defend himself against any of the them. He has fit into my crowd the most effortlessly of all of the cats I've adopted over the years.

The Sunday afternoons I spent volunteering my time at Animal Friends before I left the Pittsburgh area were some of the most rewarding of my life. Seeing the multitude of animals who were brought in as strays or discarded by their owners was heartbreaking, and it was a joy to know that in some small way I was able to help them or make their lives more enjoyable. Since that time I have volunteered for other shelters and animal organizations and have found that most of them are run by staff and volunteers who have an intense love of animals and a deep concern for their welfare, want to do what's best for them.

In the pages that follow, you will learn what makes shelter cats so special, what it takes to become a responsible pet parent, what you should know and do before bringing a pet into your home, how to choose that special cat that is meant just for you and what it will take to provide ongoing cat care. You will also learn about some of the many efforts that shelters undertake and the countless hours they spend making the animals in their care into great adoption candidates for you and pet lovers everywhere.

I live with four shelter cats, along with seven adopted as strays. I personally can vouch for shelter cats making constant companions, full of love and devotion toward their owners. Millions of them sit in shelters across the country waiting for someone special just like you to adopt them into a loving home.

CHAPTER 1

So, You Want to Adopt a Cat

Much has been written on the positive nature of the human-animal bond and how our relationship with animals can improve our overall health and well-being. The company of pets has a calming effect on us in our otherwise hurried lives. Playing with pets promotes laughter and feelings of joy and contentment. Petting an animal has been shown to reduce stress. Watching a kitten or puppy at play or investigating its world is a source of constant amusement.

Taking care of a pet has been shown to help the elderly who, without an animal's companionship, may spend many of their days alone and with no contact with other living things. Let's face it: Pets provide us with unconditional love and acceptance, regardless of our appearance, our social status or our financial situation. Pets are just as happy to see us when we come home whether we've won the lottery or lost our job.

A HOUSE IS NOT A HOME . . .

Among the animals domesticated since man first came out of the forest and into the sunlight, the cat stands out as an animal that can provide all the benefits of pet ownership while remaining at the lower end of the maintenance scale among household pets. Although cats need exercise, a cat owner will never have to fence in the backyard to provide the cat with a space in which to run, jump and play. Cats have a reputation for cleanliness, and although you will have to help your indoor cat in the grooming department, you will never have to take her to a Saturday morning pet wash or hose her down after a romp in the mud.

If you are thinking about adopting a cat, you probably know already how wonderful living with one can be. Perhaps you had a cat in your past, or perhaps a co-worker who has one talks incessantly about how wonderful his cat is. Perhaps you have a friend whose cat showers you with affection or provides you with hours of enjoyment every time you visit. If you have had any of these experiences, you already know what the fuss is about and why cats are so popular as companions.

Petting a cat and listening to her purr is as comforting as being enveloped in a favorite sweater or as soothing as listening to the patter of summer rain against the window. Listening to a cat purring has been shown to lower blood pressure and reduce the heart rate. Feeling the unique vibration under a cat's skin when sitting with one can lull her human companion into a sense of calm and tranquility that is unrivaled by the presence of any other creature.

Each cat is as individual as a flake of snow. Cats demand little and yet give so much. The presence of a cat in the home adds a dimension of grace, dignity and beauty that might not otherwise be experienced or imagined.

THE ROAD TO DOMESTICATION

Today's cat can be traced at least as far back as ancient Egypt, roughly 5,000 years ago, when the small African wildcat (*Felis lybica*) was domesticated as a household companion and protector of the Egyptian granaries from mice and other rodents. Egyptian cats were associated with gods, and their images adorned art and architecture. Open any text on ancient Egypt, and you'll find lots of images of cats adorning Egypt's art and statues of the Egyptian goddess, Bastet, envisioned in the body of a cat.

The Egyptian housecat was a little larger than today's domestic short-haired cat. Mummified remains of cats have been found buried along

Cats and people form loving, long-lasting relationships. (Photo courtesy of the San Francisco SPCA.)

with their owners. Although this practice seems to indicate a real love for their feline companions, you must realize that the cats most likely did not die by chance exactly when their owners did and that they were sacrificed specifically to be mummified and interred with the royal remains.

From Egypt, cats were imported to Greece and Rome, and on their conquests, the Romans spread cats throughout Europe. Contributing to the gene pool of *Felis catus* were the African jungle cat (*Felis chaus*) and the European wildcat (*Felis silvestris*). Although the African wildcat and the African jungle cat had subdued tabby markings, it was the European wildcat that contributed the dark tabby markings we have come to associate today with the domestic shorthair in all its iterations.

It is from those three ancestors that all of today's domestic cats, including the thirty-some breeds, arose. So, regardless of its outward appearance, every cat is a tabby at heart, and regardless of what you call it, every alley cat has the same ancestors as the most lofty and expensive purebred. When you adopt a domestic shorthaired cat from a shelter, you are adopting a descendent from the wellspring of the sacred cat of ancient Egypt.

Since the cat entered the lives of humans, she has been looked upon in a variety of ways—revered as a god, valued as a mouser, despised as an incarnation of the devil or pampered as a member of the family. Through it all, cats have retained a reputation, although undeservedly, of being the solitary hunter, independent and aloof—the pet that was put out the back door at night to find its own food and fend for itself until the first rays of sunlight at dawn permitted it once again a place in front of the hearth.

Ask cat owners these days, and you will find them testifying to the fact that cats are devoted, loving, affectionate and perfectly content to live the good life indoors with their owners. Most cats have willingly cast aside the innate desire to hunt, demanding instead that their food be offered to them from an aluminum can, a cardboard box, a wax-coated bag or a foil packet. Cats, like their human owners, know a good thing when they see it. As our lifestyles have changed, so, thankfully, has the lifestyle of the cat.

In the 1980s, cats overtook dogs as the number-one pet in America and now occupy more than 67 million homes. Cats are more easily cared for, and they are fun to observe. Bring a cat into your home, and you will find yourself spending hours just watching in amazement and wonder at the creative, amusing and sometimes silly things she does. Cat watching is the twentieth-century antidote to stress, boredom and television tedium.

THE SHELTER CAT

There is no shortage of cats in the world. Prospective pet parents can adopt cats from a variety of sources—from friends and neighbors, breeders, pet stores and shelters. In some cases, cats that have been living on the streets or in the wild will find these people, claiming an owner in the same way an owner may claim a cat.

Millions of cats find their way into shelters across the country every year. Some are strays that have been trapped or captured by people attempting to offer them a better life. Others are relinquished by their owners for any number of reasons. Still others may be from litters born to unspayed females.

Unlike dogs, whose owners are more quick to look for them when they become lost, cats are often viewed as being contented living outside. A cat may disappear for days before an owner realizes that the animal is not just having a hot time on the town and may actually be gone. Believing that the cat is outside just doing what comes naturally is a fatal assumption that many cat owners make when their cats disappear. The Humane Society of the United States estimates that of the millions of dogs and cats entering shelters each year, 14 percent of the dogs are returned to their owners, while the same pleasant outcome applies to only 4 percent of the cats. Although many of the cats you will find in shelters may

People who want to adopt a cat will find plenty of domestic shorthairs at their local animal shelter— such as Caesar, who was adopted from Animal Friends, Inc., in Pittsburgh. (Photo courtesy of Animal Friends, Inc.)

simply be pets that have wandered off and have been picked up by someone thinking they are strays, no one ever comes to claim the vast majority of them. In some respects, today's cat hasn't come very far.

Most of the cats you will find in shelters are *domestic shorthairs*. Domestic shorthairs are occasionally called *alley cats*, alluding to their common backgrounds, or *random breeds*, indicating that a real mix of ancestors contributed to their heritage. The term *domestic shorthair* is a blanket term that also includes the longer-haired versions of random-breed cats.

The domestic shorthaired cat should not be confused with the American shorthair and British shorthair breeds. Although these two breeds resemble the domestic shorthair, they are bred to have specific looks and features. The domestic shorthaired cat most cat lovers have come to know and appreciate is often included in breeding programs to strengthen the gene pool of purebred cats and to prevent weaknesses from developing due to generations of inbreeding.

WHY GO TO A SHELTER?

As a companion, a shelter cat will provide you with the same enjoyment and fun as a cat from any other source. A shelter cat will offer the same love and affection as an expensive purebred cat or a cat from a pet store.

A lot of time and effort on the part of animal shelters, their staffs and volunteers, are expended to make each and every cat in their care a good adoption candidate for you and pet lovers everywhere. When you adopt a cat from a good shelter, you will acquire a package deal that includes not just your new cat companion, but also these benefits:

- The result of countless hours of work that occurred before the adoption to make your cat into an animal capable of becoming a valued member of your family.

- The knowledge of your cat's history, behavior and medical condition.

- Additional medical care provided by the shelter while your cat stayed there.

- A commitment from the shelter to help make sure the relationship you have with your cat is a lasting one.

- *If you qualify*, financial help to enable you to provide the best possible care for your cat on an ongoing basis.

Shelters make no profit from you if you adopt one of their animals. The contribution you make at the time of adoption goes to provide continued care for the animals that come to them. Shelter staffs, regardless of whether they are paid staff members or volunteers at the organization, will want you to find the cat that is right for you and help ensure that you are committed to her continued care.

People often ask why, when so many animals cannot find homes, shelters don't simply give them away. It is important to remember that shelters need money to operate, and often they receive no tax dollars to assist them, relying solely on donations. The shelter may have a permanent staff that must be paid. The building housing the animals and support services must be heated and maintained. The animals must be fed.

If the animals are sick, they must have veterinary medical attention. Maintaining a shelter is not cost-free.

Shelters often act as the cruelty-investigation arm of local governments and municipalities, which means that investigators must be paid and trucks maintained. The investigations may result in legal action that requires the shelter staff to pursue the offender through the courts. All of this costs money, and even if shelters receive tax support, imagine how difficult it would be if they recouped none of their costs when people adopted animals from them. In addition, requiring that someone make a donation at the time of adoption is one way to weed out those people who are not serious about making a commitment to an animal.

You may have spotted notices in the Classifieds section of your local newspaper saying that it will not accept ads for *free* cats or dogs. There are those people who, when faced with the need to provide a meal for a pet boa constrictor or other exotic animal, will seize the opportunity to pick up some free kittens for their pet's daily or weekly rations. Individuals may earn a living by picking up free animals and reselling them to laboratories for experimental purposes. As painful as it is to think about, those practices are common. So, when shelters charge you a fee for adopting a cat, they are helping to prevent some of the horrible fates that can befall free animals.

CATS NEED CARE

If you are considering adopting a cat, you will be embarking on an adventure that will be an emotionally rewarding one. But before you take the plunge into cat ownership, there are some questions about yourself and your lifestyle you must answer to help make your relationship with your future pet a satisfying and lasting one for both of you.

Cats are not disposable creatures. One of the reasons why so many cats are available at shelters is that they are considered disposable by many of the people who adopt them. Leaving cats outside to run unspayed or unneutered to bear young who also will bear young, discarding them at the first sign of change in their lifestyles or simply not considering them to be permanent and valued members of the household are just some of the reasons for the revolving door of adoption and disposal that results in cats being taken from shelters and brought back again. When you adopt a cat, you should be offering her a permanent home, not a temporary one. Before you jump into the world of cat ownership, carefully weigh the decision and make sure that it is right for you.

One of the first things you should consider before adopting a cat is your financial situation. It may seem mercenary to think of adopting a pet in monetary terms, but not considering cat-care costs before you adopt may leave you feeling financially strapped or resenting your pet if she requires more of your income than you anticipated.

Although there are lots of cost-saving measures you will learn once you bring a cat into your home and begin to read up on how to care for her, you still will need to pay for cat food and other necessities as well as ongoing veterinary medical care to help ensure that your new companion lives a long and healthy life. Despite the cat's reputation for independence, your new cat will depend completely on you to provide all those things.

The *American Veterinary Medical Association*, the professional organization for veterinarians, estimates that the average cat owner will spend more than $50.00 annually on veterinary bills. That includes an office visit for an annual checkup, appropriate vaccinations (including one to prevent rabies) and other miscellaneous costs associated with keeping a cat healthy. Any sudden or long-term illness or accident requiring that your cat have additional veterinary care, emergency care, surgery or hospitalization will necessitate a financial commitment over and above the basic ongoing costs. Chapter 6, "Cat Care Basics," will discuss ways in which you can save money on your cat's health care as well as ways to set aside money in case of veterinary emergencies. Regardless, you must be prepared to provide that care despite the cost.

One of the most important things you will do for your cat is to have her spayed or him neutered. By doing so, you reduce the risk of certain kinds of cancer, prevent the birth of unwanted kittens and keep your pet from engaging in annoying mating behavior. For every cat you bring into the world, even those you find homes for, another cat will die somewhere unwanted. Spaying and neutering your cat will be beneficial all the way around. Spaying a female cat may cost anywhere from $45.00 to $120.00, depending on what part of the country you live in and whether the cat is *in heat* (ovulating) when she is spayed. Neutering a male will cost between $20.00 and $50.00.

Shelters that do not perform this operation on cats before they are adopted out will insist that you, as the new owner, have it done—and may require that you sign a contract stating that you will have the animal spayed or neutered when it reaches the appropriate age. More and more veterinarians are altering cats at a younger age, even at four months or less, so plan on providing your cat with this important surgery soon after you adopt her or him. Local organizations offer low-cost spaying and neutering operations or financial assistance for those who qualify, so investigate the facilities in your area if you need help funding the surgery.

As you will see in the pages to come, many shelters offer some type of financial help to certain pet owners. Free or low-cost spaying and neutering, regular health checkups and free rabies shots are but a few examples of this help. If finances are a concern for you, discuss your situation with the shelter from which you want to adopt. It may have programs or services to help you, or it may know of organizations that can help.

The Pet Food Institute, the professional organization that represents pet-food manufacturers, estimates that Americans spend in excess of $3 billion on cat food every year. That translates into between $3.00 and $8.00 that you will spend on food each week for one cat. Litter-box filler can cost from $6.00 to $12.00 a month. Add to that the one-time or few-time costs for necessities, such as a litter box (from $5.00 to $35.00), a scratching post ($10.00 to $100.00), some exercise toys ($3.00 to $15.00), grooming tools ($5.00 to $15.00) and a cat bed ($10.00 to $30.00), and your initial annual investment could be anywhere from close to $200.00 to more than $700.00, depending on how extravagant you want to be. Never mind the ongoing cost of food and litter and the unanticipated medical bills. Add to that the adoption cost, which varies from shelter to shelter, and the cost for spaying or neutering, and the financial investment builds up.

For most cat lovers, it may seem like a small price to pay for the constant love, affection and attention that your cat will provide, but it is something that a new cat owner should consider before committing to an animal that will have needs of its own that must be met.

PROFILE:
CATS' BILL OF RIGHTS

The *San Francisco Society for the Prevention of Cruelty to Animals* (SF/SPCA), one of the most active animal agencies in the country, developed a list of Cat Rights that appeared in an issue of "Animals and Ethics," a publication of the SF/SPCA's Ethical Studies Department. The various programs of this department include the Open Door Program, which deals with pets in rental housing, Community Outreach, Humane Investigations, the Feral Cat Assistance Plan and an animal advocacy help line. The Cat Rights document presents a view of the SF/SPCA's philosophy regarding cats, their place in our homes as companion animals and their place in the animal kingdom in general.

Cat Rights

The growing popularity of cats as housepets has gone hand in hand with increased efforts to legislate, regulate and even eradicate these animals from our midst. In light of this growing threat to cats' lives and welfare, we feel obligated to come forward and offer our perspective. The Cat Rights listed below represent the basic principles that have guided our efforts on behalf of cats. While each seems fundamental to us, these rights are far from settled. All except one reflect an intense controversy within the humane movement. We hope everyone will listen to all sides, participate in the debate, and reach their own conclusions—the fate of millions of cats depends on it.

The Right to be recognized as a unique and important species.

The Right to have their individual lives cherished and protected.

The Right to be free from cruelty and abuse.

The Right to receive aid and comfort, including food, water, shelter and medical care.

The Right to a fair share of public resources for the care and treatment of companion animals.

The Right to be treated as equal members of the animal kingdom.

The Right to be represented accurately and humanely by those who speak on their behalf.

The SF/SPCA devotes a great deal of time and effort working with local governments to promote cat welfare, with local agencies to increase the opportunities for pet owners who rent or may need assistance to keep their pets and with the public to educate them on responsible pet ownership.

The SF/SPCA has a four-tiered screening process that uses a corps of 800 volunteers who function as adoption counselors. They log thousands of hours trying to find the right human for each pet. After a preliminary consultation, prospective pet parents fill out a multipage questionnaire and participate in an interview with staff adoption specialists. If the pet has special needs, a medical staff member or an animal behaviorist advises the applicant on followup care or training. The screening process can take several hours, and every person who adopts is called one week after the adoption to make sure that the pet is adjusting to her new home.

People who adopt must understand and commit to the SF/SPCA's tenets of responsible pet ownership and must be completely willing to take on the extra burden of care that many pets require. Pet parents also must commit to caring for the pet for the duration of her life.

THE SPACE AGE

We are living in an era when home for many of us is no longer a single-family dwelling, but an apartment that may contain only one, two or three rooms. The spacious country farmhouses of yesteryear have been replaced by sprawling suburbs and urban high-rises. One of the factors experts attribute to the cat's increased popularity is that cats will do well in smaller living areas such as apartments or condominiums. Unlike a dog, which requires lots of room to run and exercise, a cat will find the confines of a smaller living space completely suitable to her exercise needs.

One way for cat owners living in small spaces to offer extra room for their furry companions is to make use of vertical space in their homes or apartments. Climbing apparatus, wall-mounted shelving or cat trees will expand your cat's available indoor space so that she can get plenty of exercise within your four walls, giving new meaning to the phrase *upward mobility*.

So, if you are concerned that your home may not be big enough for a cat to be comfortable, don't be. Unless you are living in a closet, your cat will be just as happy in an efficiency apartment as she will in a ten-room mansion.

IF YOU RENT

If you rent your space, however, you will need to ask your landlord if pets are allowed before you bring one home with you. Don't assume that if you see other pets in your building or apartment complex that they are there with the landlord's permission. They could be visiting, be residing unknown to the apartment management, be grandfathered in before a no-pets rule was instituted or be assistance animals in service to their owners and therefore allowed by law.

No matter how clever a cat owner thinks she is or how secretive she is about carrying the cat in and out of the apartment for veterinary care or other visits, sooner or later the cat is discovered by the landlord or a maintenance worker who comes to fix something in the apartment. If the cat sits in the window or cries, is left to run in the apartment complex grounds or hallways or is allowed to soil the grounds, a neighbor may be the one to discover the illicit feline and blow the whistle on the owner.

Nothing does more harm to you, your cat and other renters who may want to adopt a pet than to hide a cat in your apartment. So before you bring a cat into an unwelcome situation, discuss the option with your landlord. Convince him or her that you are a responsible pet owner, that the cat will be neutered or spayed, that it will remain indoors and that it will be trained not to damage property. Offer to show the landlord your cat's vaccination certificate and proof of altering. If necessary, offer the landlord a right to inspect your apartment periodically when you are there. Offer to provide a reference for your dependability and the name of a veterinarian you will use to have your cat spayed or neutered, vaccinated and examined for ongoing health care. Do everything possible to prove that you are a responsible pet owner.

If your landlord agrees to allow a pet in your apartment, get permission in writing. If your landlord is firm about not bringing a pet into your apartment, *don't even think about it.* When landlords find pets in apartments that don't allow them, it is the pet who most often suffers and must be surrendered back to a shelter or relocated to a home with a new owner.

Don't assume that because you own a condominium or the trailer in which you live that you will be able to bring a pet into it. Condominiums are governed by an association of condo residents who make the rules governing all the condo owners who reside there. People who live in trailer parks, regardless of whether they own their trailer, must abide by the rules of the trailer park. If the condo-association or trailer-park rules forbid pets, you must abide by those rules, work to change them or risk being ostracized or taken to court when your unwanted pet is discovered. Condo associations have forced goldfish and bird owners to get rid of their pets, so don't assume that because a cat is small or living completely indoors she will go unnoticed or unchallenged.

CONSIDER YOUR FAMILY OR ROOMMATES

If you live alone, the only opinion you have to consider before adopting a cat is your own or perhaps that of your landlord. Great. But if you have roommates or family members, they will need to be consulted before you bring a cat into a home that is both yours and theirs.

A cat should be wanted and welcome by every member of the household. If there is an older person in your home who does not like pets, or someone with allergies is opposed to living with a pet, it's best not to adopt until your living situation changes.

Once you determine that a cat will be a welcome addition to the family, you should designate someone to be the primary caregiver who will look after the cat's needs. An alternative is to share the tasks equally among family members. How the responsibilities will be divided should be decided up front, and who does what task and when should be determined before bringing your pet home.

If you are single and living with roommates who come and go, you will want to make sure that any present and future people who share living quarters with you will be as appreciative of your cat as you will be. Your cat will view all the members of the household as her family unit even though she belongs to you. Changes to the family unit will cause your cat just as much stress as if you were living at home and your brothers, sisters or parents came and left. If your living situation means that the members of the household will be in flux, you will want to make sure that you can keep your cat from being stressed by the situation or delay adopting a cat until your situation is more stable.

Adopting a pet should never be undertaken as a way to teach a child responsibility. The child should be deemed responsible prior to giving him or her an animal to care for. If the child's performance does not live up to the parent's expectations, both the child and the pet may suffer. If you, as a parent, were expecting your children to take care of the cat, you may be left with the job if they don't do what is required. So, before you provide Justin or Joleen with an animal to take care of, make sure that he or she is up to the task. A child can learn responsibility by being given tasks to perform related to the cat's care, but performance of these tasks should occur under your supervision. When these tasks aren't handled as necessary, someone will have to pick up the slack.

Depending on the ages of the children in your house, you may want to look for cats of certain ages or with certain personality types. For example, a kitten may not fare well in a household with very small children who do not yet know how to handle a delicate animal carefully or who, when being playful, may risk being scratched. An older or more stocky, laid-back cat might be more appropriate under such circumstances than one that is young, slender and wiry, or more active.

As when you bring any animal into the home, you should teach your children to handle cats with care, gentleness and respect. Children should give the same care to the cat as you would provide yourself. That includes allowing the animal to eat her meal in peace; not startling the cat when she is sleeping, resting, amusing herself or using the litter box and not treating her like a toy.

PROFILE:
HELPING KIDS HELP ANIMALS

To help its city's children and youth learn about animal welfare and responsible pet care, the Animal Welfare League of Alexandria, Virginia, offers a stimulating camp every summer. The Absolutely Awesome Animal Awareness Camp of Alexandria teaches children what the animal shelter does and fosters in them an appreciation of animals, their needs and their place in the environment. Children also learn about pet over-population and how they can help homeless, abandoned, abused and neglected animals in their community. Children learn to interact with animals appropriately and to become humane teachers in their own communities and with their friends.

The camp is held weekdays from 9 a.m. to 12:30 p.m. The Animal Welfare League of Alexandria holds four such sessions during the summer months, with six children at each session. So popular is the camp that available slots fill by March. The Animal Welfare League offers scholarships to students who cannot afford the registration fee of $75.00, which covers the costs of T-shirts given to campers, materials, speaker fees and supplies.

To address the increase in registrations, the league developed a second program called Animals, Animals, Animals, which is geared toward inner-city youth. It is a one-day program that is free of charge.

Children attending the Absolutely Awesome Animal Awareness Camp learn about the benefits of adopting animals from shelters. (Photo courtesy of the Animal Welfare League of Alexandria, Virginia.)

Guest speakers at the camps include representatives from animal-control agencies; wildlife-rehabilitation specialists; veterinarians; professional dog trainers; U.S. Fish and Wildlife agents, zoologists, and herpetologists and ichthyologists from the National Aquarium in Baltimore, Maryland.

Children take in-depth tours of the shelter in Alexandria and learn about its position in the community. They observe shelter workers and learn about what they do. Campers learn about spaying and neutering pets, how to take animals out of their kennels for exercise and play, proper etiquette around shelter animals, basic pet care and how a person adopts an animal. They learn about different breeds of cats and dogs, grooming, proper diet, the importance of keeping cats indoors and cat socializing. The campers engage in arts-and-crafts activities that include making T-shirts, birdhouses and frames for each camper's photo taken with a favorite pet.

The Animal Welfare League of Alexandria has been in existence for nearly fifty years. It is dedicated to placing animals in good, loving homes, reducing the pet overpopulation problem and educating the community about responsible pet ownership. The league's shelter is open seven days a week, except on major holidays.

CONSIDER YOUR OTHER PETS

If your other pets are tropical fish, you don't have to be concerned about how your fish will react. Fish don't know what cats are, so they won't be any more afraid of Fluffy approaching the aquarium than they are of you. Cats love to investigate just about everything, so the fish may be just as mesmerizing to your cat as they are to the human members of your household. Just make sure that you have a hood on your tank to protect your fish and your cat from accidents.

Similarly, if you or another family member has a small mammal as a pet, such as a gerbil or hamster, or any type of bird, make sure that your new cat is known to get along with these types of animals and that the other animal will not go into cardiac arrest when it meets the cat. If you have doubts, keep them from ever meeting one another. Cats are hunters at heart, and your small pet may look like a prime target or a toy to your cat regardless of how well you feed her or how many toys you provide.

Kittens can be raised around other types of animals and all will be perfectly safe, but if you adopt an older shelter cat whose background is unknown, it is safest to keep it away from other pets, such as rats, mice, gerbils, birds and any other animal that may look like dinner.

Cats and dogs also can get along quite well together but are best introduced to one another when they are young. Kittens and puppies raised together will have the best chance of getting along. If you have an older dog, you still have a good chance of creating a pair that will play and perhaps even bond together, especially if you know that the shelter cat previously had been in a home with a dog. You'll learn more about proper introductions in Chapter 5, "Bringing Home Baby."

SNAPSHOT:
Maggie, the Cat Who Tests Dogs

If you're thinking of bringing a cat into a household that already has a dog, wouldn't it be wonderful if you could test the relationship out on a cat ahead of time, knowing full well that absolutely no harm would come to either feline or canine? As improbable as it seems, people coming to the Pasadena Humane Society in Pasadena, California, who want to bring a cat into a household with a dog (or vice versa) can pretest the relationship by introducing the canine in question to Maggie, the resident cat. Among her other duties, Maggie meets dogs to see if the relationship might work.

Maggie was found as a tiny kitten in 1990 in a Pasadena dumpster. The gray-and-brown tabby was brought to the Pasadena Humane Society, where she was acclimated to life with humans. As a permanent shelter resident, she also apparently acclimated herself to life with dogs and made lots of mental notes about which ones were good company and which ones weren't. She can tell in a tail's wag if a dog will like her and if she will like him. People thinking about a new relationship with a member of the opposite sex should have her instincts.

Maggie has what Executive Director Steve McNall calls an *enhanced personality*, which enables her to give a paws up or paws down to an impending trans-species relationship. Her reaction, and that of the dog, help owners or prospective owners determine ahead of time how a dog will react in the presence of a cat. Introductions occur slowly, with the dog under complete control at all times. Maggie has free run of the shelter's Humane Education Department and Volunteer Action Center and is free to leave the conference room where introductions occur at a moment's notice if the dog offends her sensibilities and appears threatening. She also has her claws intact, but more often than not doesn't need to use them. "You can tell by a dog's behavior if it is not cat-friendly," says McNall. "As soon as the dog comes into the room, his nose picks up the scent of a cat in the room. You can tell by the body language of the dog if the dog, in fact, will be somewhat aggressive or will be a little bit more than normally active in pursuing the cat."

The strict screening process at the Pasadena Humane Society includes on-staff adoption counselors who try to match

Maggie helps prospective pet owners determine if a dog is cat-friendly. (Photo courtesy of the Pasadena Humane Society.)

the right people with the right pet. They make sure that every member of the family visits the shelter to interact with prospective pets. If the family has a dog and wants to bring a cat into the household, the dog must come to the shelter to meet Maggie. If the family has a cat and wants to adopt a dog, the shelter dog must first meet Maggie. The stringent process helps the shelter reduce the return rate of animals who, for one reason or another, come back because the new home situation did not work out. "It's to help us," says McNall. "We don't like to deny an adoption, but we sure don't like the revolving-door approach, either. You can't put a price tag on these animals, so what we try to do is make it a one-time adoption."

Maggie assists with that effort.

Cats are likely to get along with other cats, especially if they have lived in multi-cat environments. Their reputation for being solitary creatures is undeserved, and studies are being done that point to their social nature. Feral colonies, multi-cat households, cageless shelters and barnyard situations are prime examples of situations in which cats do quite well socially. They form packs, develop friendships and form smaller social structures within the larger group setting.

A new cat in your home has a good chance of getting along with a cat or cats that you already have. To help increase your chances, select a cat known to have been with other cats in her past, or go to a cageless shelter where you will find cats that already have been socialized with other felines.

A LIFETIME OF LOVE

Back in the dark ages of feline history, when cats spent their days outdoors hunting and scavenging for their daily rations, the life span of the average cat was seven years or less. Today, thanks to advances in feline nutrition and veterinary medicine, that figure has dramatically increased. When you adopt a cat, you will be embarking on a relationship that will last for many years. Before you adopt, consider your living situation. Is it likely to change in the near future, and if it does, will your cat be a part of it?

In the late twentieth century, change is the cornerstone of our existence, and our favorite feline can adapt well to that change if attention is given to her to make it a positive experience. Drastic change, such as moving to a new home, upheaval in the household or loss or gain of family members, can be stressful for a cat. But nothing is more traumatic for a cat than to find that she loses her loving owner and comfortable home and is taken back to a shelter in the hopes that she will find a new one. The tragic truth is that most do not.

Shelters are overstocked with cats whose owners offer excuses for giving them up such as, "I'm moving and can't take him with me," or "I just got married and my spouse doesn't like cats," or "I'm having a baby and won't have time for a cat." If you are anticipating making some changes in your life, carefully consider if the cat you want to adopt will be going along with you. If you doubt it, consider adopting a cat later when your situation is more stable.

THE TIME OF YOUR LIFE

Another fact that experts attribute to the growing popularity of cats is that keeping a cat does not pose a significant conflict with our busy lifestyles. Because cats are capable of and willing to manage their bodily functions on their own, you will not have to get up at 5 a.m. to walk your cat, nor will you have to worry about your cat's potty habits on evenings when you must work late. Your cat will be perfectly content to use her own bathroom facilities before you wake up in the morning or you arrive home at night.

Cats do need attention and companionship, however, so if you find that your lifestyle or your job requires that you spend long days at the office regularly or just away from home, you might want to adopt two cats at the same time to provide that extra bit of companionship for your cat during the hours you are not there. Many shelters offer special fees

Busy people might want to consider adopting two kittens or cats to serve as companions for each other, such as these two littermates at the San Francisco SPCA. (Photo courtesy of the San Francisco SPCA.)

for someone who is willing to adopt more than one cat at a time. Occasionally, you will find cats at shelters that have come from the same home and would be only too willing to find another home in which they could spend their time together. Splitting up cats that are accustomed to being with each other can be traumatic, so if you have room in your home, think about a second cat if you are constantly on the go.

A second cat companion is no substitute for you, however, so provide your cat, or cats, with lots of kisses and hugs when you're home and a pet-sitter if you are away overnight.

PETS AS GIFTS

As wonderful as adopting a cat or other animal is, pets make lousy gifts. Selecting the right cat is a personal experience that can only be undertaken by the person who will live with him or her. Bonding can only take place between the person and cat in question. No one can do it for them. It may take weeks of shopping at local shelters before a person finds the right cat. If the cat is for a young member of the household, he or she should be a part of the shopping expedition and the selection process. By involving the child in the selection, you will be helping to ensure his or her continued involvement with the pet's care.

In addition to the personal nature of selecting a pet, certain times of the year are just the wrong times to adopt an animal. Christmas is a popular time for thinking about giving a pet as a gift, but the holiday season is so hectic that the gift recipient may not have time to get to know the animal, much less train her to become a pleasant member of the household. A new pet in the household may be temporarily forgotten when other holiday activities occupy a person's time.

If you are thinking of giving a cat as a gift to someone who you know *definitely* wants to adopt one, why not assemble a box or basket of cat-care items that the person could use for a new feline? Cat toys, grooming tools and supplies, cat food and treats, a litter scoop and litter liners are but a few of the items you could include. Pack them inside a litter box and present them to the prospective cat owner.

Another appropriate animal-related gift idea is to go to a local shelter and obtain a gift certificate for the amount of the donation it requires at the time of adoption. Or obtain a spay or neuter certificate from a veterinarian or a spay/neuter organization. Offer to take the person to the shelter after the holiday or special occasion and help him or her select and transport the cat. Or offer to take the new pet parent and the cat to the veterinarian when it is time for the spay or neuter operation. Provide a certificate of your own making that entitles your friend to a case of cat food that the new cat likes to eat, or offer to help shop for kitty supplies.

If you know a person who would like to adopt a cat, helping make the adoption process more convenient or helping with the care of the animal on an ongoing basis will be a thoughtful and welcome gift from you. There's no limit to the number of things you could do, other than giving a pet as a gift, for your pet-loving friends or relatives.

CHAPTER 2

What Kind of Cat Do You Want?

You've thought about bringing a cat into your home, carefully considered the commitment and now you've decided that adopting one is the right move for you. Fantastic! Chapter 1, "So, You Want to Adopt a Cat," described your responsibilities as a new pet owner and some of the things you will need to do to care for your new cat. Now that you've decided you are willing to make the commitment to a cat just waiting at a shelter for someone like you to come along, you will want to begin thinking about what kind of cat you want.

Shelters cry out for people who are willing to adopt the many cats that come to them. In a study conducted by the National Council on Pet Population, a group of animal-related organizations that included the Humane Society of the United States, it was estimated that of the 4.3 million animals entering shelters every year, 1.6 million were cats. Of those, only 22.6 percent were adopted. More than 71 percent of them were euthanized. Unfortunately, most of the cats you will meet at shelters will be put to death because of a lack of homes for them.

As you journey from shelter to shelter looking at the wonderful cats residing in them, it will be hard for you to choose just one cat. Sadly, you will have to face the fact that you just can't save all of them, no matter how much you would like to. Picking a single feline (or a pair, if you decide that one cat in your busy lifestyle should have a companion) out of the hundreds you'll meet will be one of the hardest decisions you will have to make. Spend some time before you take the first step toward a shelter door thinking about the kind of cat you want to share your home. A little planning will help you make the right selection and prevent you from having to live with a cat that is not suited to you or your lifestyle.

Adorable cats such as Nick await adoption at Animal Friends, Inc., in Pittsburgh, Pennsylvania. (Photo courtesy of Margaret G. Stanley, Animal Friends, Inc.)

THE GROWTH STAGES OF A CAT'S LIFE

Kittens

Everyone loves kittens—cute, cuddly, playful, energetic and a joy to watch as they explore their worlds. Shelters have little, if any, trouble finding homes for healthy kittens. For a good many prospective pet parents, a kitten represents an animal that can be taught and trained and that can adapt to its new home more easily than an older cat. Kittens are often looked upon, whether rightly or wrongly, as less likely to come with bad habits and health problems due to previously bad diets or a lack of medical care.

If you have your heart set on adopting a kitten, talk to the staff at your local shelter about the kittens it has available. Find out, if possible, where the kittens came from. Were they feral? Did they come from a pet owner who simply did not get her own cat spayed? Were the cats fostered to become accustomed to being around people? In Chapter 3, "Selecting a Shelter," you'll learn more about fostering and what it may mean to you as a prospective cat owner.

There is no shortage of kittens at shelters across the country, like these at Animal Friends, Inc. (Photo courtesy of Margaret G. Stanley, Animal Friends, Inc.)

Even if the kittens were feral and not socialized a great deal, it does not mean they will not make great pets. You just need to be aware that it may require some extra time, attention and patience on your part to acclimate your feral kitten to your home. If you decide to do so, you will be rewarded with the same love, affection and attention you would receive from any other cat.

If you adopt a kitten, be prepared to provide plenty of outlets for his highly charged energy. Also be prepared to spend time training a kitten to behave in ways that are appropriate to life indoors with humans. A kitten will exhibit many play behaviors that help him learn to deal with his world in feline terms. Play biting, play aggression, running and climbing and predatory behaviors like pouncing and attacking will help him learn the skills he would need as an adult if he were to live outside.

But your kitten must adjust to life in your house, so the natural behaviors in which he engages will need to be modified for him to become a satisfactory companion animal. Chapter 7, "Basic Training," will address training and behavior modification.

Kittens begin to dig in loose material at the age of about four weeks. This predisposes them to burying their waste, and kittens will naturally gravitate toward a litter box if it is provided. Training your kitten to use one may be as simple as placing him in the box.

Your kitten will learn socialization skills during his first two to three months of life, whether it be socializing with you as his human companion or other pets that reside in your home.

Like all cats, your new kitten will have special dietary needs, so you will need to provide him with food that has been developed specifically to meet a kitten's requirements for growth. Health care and nutrition will be discussed more fully in Chapter 6, "Cat Care Basics."

Adult Cats

If a more laid-back, easygoing feline is your cup of catnip tea, you might want to seriously consider adopting an adult cat. Shelters are full of adult cats that would make good pets for anyone committed to their care. The older a cat is when he comes to a shelter, the more difficult he is to place with a new owner.

Cats are considered adult when they reach sexual maturity at anywhere from six to twelve months of age. An adult cat will develop secondary sexual characteristics. In a male, these include fuller hair around the neck and a more pronounced jowl line. If unaltered, an adult cat will begin to display more territorial mating behavior. Spaying or neutering your cat prior to sexual maturity will prevent such behavior from occurring in your home. You'll learn more about that later in this chapter.

Just because a cat is an adult does not mean that he will not play. Cats play throughout their lives, even as seniors, so don't think that because you've adopted an adult cat, he will just lie around the house all day like Garfield waiting for you to run the can opener.

Your adult cat will want to become involved in your activities, whether you are sitting on the sofa reading the newspaper or sitting at the computer balancing your checkbook. These activities interest the adult cat simply because you, as his caregiver, are doing them. Adult cats establish a special bond with their owners, perhaps because they have been taken from the stressful shelter environment or because they simply are so willing to offer love and affection.

Adult cats offer just as much love and companionship as kittens, and their calmer dispositions may be more suitable to some prospective pet parents. (Photo courtesy of Karen Commings.)

You've heard that there's no truth to the saying *You can't teach an old dog new tricks*. Well, there's no truth to the notion that you can't teach an old cat, either. Adult cats are just as capable of learning how to behave in your household as a kitten. In fact, your adult shelter cat may come trained in many areas of behavior that already make him capable of being a suitable indoor companion. So, instead of spending your time running around cleaning up after an energetic kitten, you can spend your time petting and playing with a well-behaved adult. If some behaviors are not suitable, you can retrain your cat as well. If you are looking for a companion that will want to spend his days and nights in your company instead of climbing your curtains, the adult cat is for you.

Just like kittens, adult cats require regular medical care, including an annual checkup and vaccinations. If your cat has not been altered by the shelter, you should do so as soon as possible before he develops habits, such as spraying, associated with territorial marking and mating. You may want to discuss with your veterinarian the best foods to feed your adult cat. Many varieties are on the market, and your veterinarian can help you choose the best ones for the needs of your special cat.

Seniors

Even though cats are living longer these days, a seven- or eight-year-old cat is still considered to be a senior by most animal experts. You may have a hard time distinguishing a senior cat from an adult by outward appearance or by activity level. For a senior cat coming to a shelter, the likelihood of adoption is poor. Shelters have an incredibly difficult time placing senior cats. Unfortunately for these loving felines, most potential pet parents would rather adopt a kitten or even a younger adult cat than a cat they feel will only be with them for a few years (even though those years may total a decade or more).

There are many good reasons to adopt a senior cat. By interacting with the cat at a shelter, you will get a good feel for his personality and whether the two of you can establish an emotional bond. Although senior cats can be trained just like a young kitten, the senior personality is more set and predictable than that of a younger cat. A senior cat will want to play as a younger cat does, although he may want to sleep a little longer during the day. A senior cat will want to spend as much time with you as a younger cat will and will be fully capable of offering love and companionship for a very long time. And with good veterinary care and appropriate nutrition, your senior cat companion will spend many good years with you.

A senior cat may be less able than a younger cat to handle stress caused by sudden changes in environment or diet. If you are anticipating such changes, it's best to ease your senior cat into them gradually or to make environmental changes as stress-free as possible by giving your cat extra attention during the time of change and afterward.

As a cat ages, the costs for veterinary care may rise, too. As with any animal, including the human animal, more things can go wrong with the body as it grows older. At the age of ten or above (or perhaps sooner, if you detect health problems), your cat should have regular blood work to check the condition of his kidneys, liver, thyroid and so on. By observing your older cat closely and paying attention to his behavior and how it may change, you will be able to detect health problems when they begin. Regular checkups and additional blood work annually will help reduce the development of life-threatening, untreatable or financially unmanageable health problems.

As your senior cat ages, his nutritional requirements will change. As his energy level decreases, he will need food with less fat and fewer carbohydrates. Eating a little less may be a solution to his decreasing activity level, but discuss any changes in your cat's diet with your veterinarian beforehand.

SNAPSHOT:
Josie

When cat lover Melanie Bogardus headed to the Helen Opperman Krause Animal Foundation, Inc.'s shelter, she intended to adopt a kitten as a companion for herself and her three-year-old cat, Nancy Drew. After looking at a lot of cats, Bogardus lifted a sad-looking, ten-year-old tabby named Josie out of her cage in the shelter's infirmary room.

Josie put her paws around Bogardus' neck, and Bogardus fell in love with her immediately. Even though Josie had runny eyes and was on medication, Bogardus decided to adopt her. They developed a very special bond.

"I don't know what her history was," says Bogardus, "but she used to cringe when I first tried to pet her. Now she's come out of her shell."

In addition to her runny eyes, Josie developed some kidney problems. The veterinarian put her on a special diet developed for cats with kidney dysfunction, and now Josie is eating just fine.

Senior shelter cat, Josie, relaxes at her new home. (Photo courtesy of Melanie Bogardus.)

Nancy Drew adjusted to having Josie as a housemate. Although Nancy Drew wouldn't purr for a while after Bogardus adopted Josie, her motor began running again after about a year of silence. The two cats now sleep near one another and engage in mutual grooming on occasion.

"Josie is such a wonderful cat," says Bogardus. "Nancy Drew is my fun cat that's always ready for a game with anyone. Josie gives me her silent love and constant support."

For Bogardus, the fact that Josie was ten years old when she adopted her made no difference in her selection. If anything, Josie's age might have helped her decide to make her a part of the family. "There are so many adult cats at shelters," says Bogardus. "If someone would take them home, they would see how nice they are."

SEX AND SIZE

Cat owners will always disagree on which makes a better pet—a male cat or a female cat. In a multiple-cat household, you might be able to point to a typically male versus female personality or behavior in that setting, but if you are looking for one special cat to bring home, its sex won't make too much difference.

A cat, once it is sexually mature, will begin to exhibit territorial behavior that is associated with reproduction. Male cats are no more territorial than females, however, and a female that has had a litter of kittens is more likely to establish and defend a territory than is a male.

If your male cat has not been neutered, you may find him spraying (scent marking) objects in your home once he arrives at puberty (six to twelve months of age). If there are no other cats in the house and none hanging around outside that are unaltered, a male cat kept indoors may not feel compelled to spray to mark territory even if he is older. Because you cannot control the presence of cats outside your home that can trigger spraying from your indoor cat, it's best to neuter him as soon as your veterinarian feels he is of age.

If your female cat is not spayed before coming into heat (ovulating), she may engage in sexually suggestive behavior that is loud and annoying to anyone but a male cat. Female cats have been known to spray just like their male counterparts, so don't think that because you've brought home a female, you are safe from spraying to mark territory. As mentioned earlier, spaying and neutering will prevent this behavior as well as health problems such as ovarian or mammary cancer.

Unlike dogs, whose sizes can range from Chihuahuas to Great Danes, the size of cats does not vary much. Male cats, as a rule, are a little larger than females, but that is not always true. A female Maine Coon probably will outsize a male Siamese or Burmese, but the cats you will find at a shelter are seldom recognizable as particular breeds. More will be said about this in Chapter 8, "If You Really Want a Breed." Among shelter cats, size is not dependent on the sex of the animal. If you've selected an adult or senior cat, you will immediately know his size, but you will not be able to predict the size a kitten will become when he reaches adulthood. Even if you know who his parents were, their size is no guarantee of the size of their offspring.

THE HAIR'S THE THING

Shelter cats come in the shorthaired variety and the longhaired variety. Among the shorthaired cats, some have sleek hair that lays close against their bodies. Others have thicker hair with dense undercoats. This hair will eventually stick on you, your clothes, your carpet and your furniture, regardless of the type of cat you adopt. Cats with thick or long hair may shed a little more, but it is likely that a sleek-haired cat will leave deposits of hair on you and your furniture, too. Whatever type of cat you adopt, expect it to shed to some degree. If you're thinking about selecting a shelter cat that won't shed, forget it. There is no such animal.

Cats with sleek hair are generally easier to groom than their longhaired and thicker-haired counterparts, which may require more time in the grooming department. If you do not keep up with grooming for these two types of cats, you will find Fluffy not just fluffy but also matted. Once a cat's hair becomes matted, it may require the efforts of a professional groomer to return it to its former beauty and luster. If the problem is severe, the coat may need to be shaved off, which may require anesthetizing the cat. Shelters are constantly faced with cats coming to them whose only problem is that they need to be brushed.

Another outcome of not grooming your cat regularly is the development of *hairballs*—quantities of hair your cat ingests when he washes himself. If not prevented or treated properly, hairballs can become quite large and lodge in your cat's digestive tract, occasionally requiring surgery to remove. So whatever type of cat you select, plan on grooming him at least once a week and more often if his hair warrants it.

There is no correlation between the length of a cat's coat and whether or not it will affect someone who has allergies. All cats have *dander*—microscopic particles that may cause an allergic reaction in some individuals, particularly those who have breathing problems such as asthma. Some cats seem to have more dander than others, so if you or someone in your household has an allergy to cat dander, you might want to bring the affected person with you when you select a cat. Spend some extra time with each cat available at a shelter before choosing one to determine which one might affect you the least or not at all.

Believe it or not, there is a type of cat that has no hair. Called the Sphynx, it has the appearance of being completely bald, although some fine down may cover its body. There are also a few types of cats that have short, curly hair, such as the Cornish Rex and the Devon Rex. Emanating originally from Great Britain, these two curly-haired breeds were developed from spontaneous mutations. These breeds of cats are said to be more manageable for people with allergies, but it is extremely unlikely that you will ever find any of these three breeds of cats in a shelter.

Coat Color

Shelter cats come in all colors and combinations of colors—solid-color cats, bi-color (two-tone), multicolor, tabby, or tabby and white. If you look closely, even at a solid-colored cat, you may notice very slightly-colored stripes, particularly in the tail, indicating the cat's wild heritage.

As a new cat owner, you most likely will not need to know the genetic background of various coat colors and patterns, but you may be interested to know that some of the combinations of colors on cats are so charismatic and arresting that they have been given names.

Calico

A cat that has a three-colored coat consisting of red (what most of us think of as orange but is called red by folks in the cat fancy) and black patches on white is called a calico. The gene that changes a black coat color to red and creates the colorful patches is sex-linked, which means that almost all calico cats are female. It is estimated that only one in 3,000 calico cats is a male, and he will be sterile, making him unable to reproduce. Calico cats are thought to bring good luck.

The origin of the word *calico* is uncertain. It may have come from the city of Calcutta, India, where colorful calico fabric was made. In Japan, small figurines of calico cats often grace the home.

Tortoiseshell

A tortoiseshell cat has the same coat colors as a calico except that, instead of bold patches of color, the tortie coat colors are mottled, appearing as though an artist has flecked the coat with light brush strokes of color. Japanese sailors setting out to sea chose a tortoiseshell cat for good fortune to accompany them on their journey.

Tuxedo

One of the most handsome and comical-looking cats is the tuxedo. Tuxedos have black bodies with white feet, white bibs, white whiskers and white splotches on their faces. The white feet and bibs make them look as if they are dressed for a formal occasion—hence the name *tuxedo*. The spluttering cartoon character Sylvester gave the tuxedo cat a personality to match his appearance with his comical onscreen antics. Another tuxedo, Socks, the First Feline, has attracted Democratic and Republican cat lovers alike during the Clinton administration.

Tabby

Tabby cats are the most numerous and popular cats in the United States today. Tabbies come in four basic coat patterns: the mackerel or striped pattern, the classic blotched pattern, the spotted tabby and the Abyssinian or ticked tabby.

Morris, the red tabby spokescat for 9-Lives™ pet food, turned finicky eating habits into an art form and made the tabby cat popular. The current Morris is really the third tabby to play that role. Morris and his two predecessors were adopted from shelters.

When you visit a local shelter, you will find lots of tabby cats in an assortment of colors and coat patterns available for adoption. Some will have the white spotting gene, making the hair on their feet and other parts of their body white, along with the tabby markings.

The Healthy Cat

Most shelters will attempt to isolate cats that are obviously suffering from contagious diseases, such as upper-respiratory problems, from those cats that appear to be healthy. If the shelter has enough space, all cats will be isolated when they first arrive until they can be examined for any problems that could be passed to other cats in the shelter. The Helen Opperman Krause Animal Foundation, Inc., for example, has a separate hospital ward where sick animals are brought back to health before they enter the cat facility where they are visited by the public.

Temporary isolation is particularly important for cageless shelters or those that keep all or groups of cats in communal areas. If cats are not isolated until they are deemed healthy, diseases can spread like wildfire, and pretty soon all the cats in the communal area will be showing signs of illness. Not only does that decrease the likelihood of a cat being adopted, but it increases the long-term costs of the shelter when it is forced to medicate dozens or even hundreds of cats instead of only a few.

If the shelter can afford it, it will have new arrivals tested for some of the more devastating contagious diseases—such as *feline leukemia virus* (FeLV) or *feline immunodeficiency virus* (FIV)—before putting them up for adoption. Cats known to be carriers will remain isolated and adopted out to cat owners who are willing to care for them despite the added medical attention and expense they require or who have other cats suffering from the same conditions.

It is good advice for first-time cat owners to look for a healthy cat instead of adopting one known to have health problems. Most cats that are placed up for adoption by a shelter already have been treated for any health problems they might have, so most cats you will find will qualify. Occasionally, shelters have available for adoption cats with conditions such as FeLV or FIV. Although cats with such conditions may not show any outward signs of illness and may live a long time, you should know beforehand what to expect and what it may require of you as a pet parent to care for such a cat. A good place to start is by talking to shelter personnel or veterinarians before deciding to adopt a cat with either of these conditions.

Healthy cats will appear alert, have bright, clear eyes with no discharge and have a coat that appears clean and well-groomed. A coat that is matted does not necessarily indicate that a cat has a health problem—the cat's previous owner may not have groomed him regularly. Such a problem is easily remedied by some regular, proper coat care. A cat that is sick, however, will stop washing, his coat will become dull and clumped and he will appear listless and generally disinterested in what is going on around him.

Alaska's only problem was that she needed someone to make her healthy for prospective pet parents to want to bring home. (Photo courtesy of the San Francisco SPCA.)

Cats suffering from illnesses or physical problems or disabilities still make good, loving pets, but you need to know that they might require extra veterinary attention, extra expenditures and extra care to restore them to health. If you bond with a cat that is not in peak condition, he will provide you with all the love that a healthy cat can, but he will need more time and attention from you to make him healthy.

Don't assume that because a cat cowers in the back of his cage or that because he does not appear very active that there is something wrong with him. Shelters can be frightening for cats for a number of reasons—they are in unfamiliar surroundings, they are handled by strangers, they hear noises from dogs and other cats, they detect unfamiliar smells and they see people coming in and viewing them all day. No matter how sensitive the shelter staff and volunteers are to their needs, from a cat's point of view, being in a shelter can be a pretty scary experience, especially if the cat came from a home in which he felt loved and secure. A timid cat might be just that—timid. Such an animal will make a loving member of your home. Sometimes all it takes is getting the cat out of the shelter and into your house. You simply may need to provide an extra portion of tender loving care to bring him out of his shell.

THE PERSONABLE CAT

Although cats may not be very different in size or have different personalities based on their sex, the one thing that all cat owners can agree on is that no two cats are alike. Each and every one exhibits his own unique personality. Some are comical and bring their owners to fits of

PROFILE:
ADOPTION PACT SAVES LIVES

Every year, thousands of animals have been euthanized at San Francisco's Animal Control Center. To help alleviate the suffering and untimely deaths of these animals that have the potential to become someone's beloved pet, the San Francisco SPCA and the San Francisco Department of Animal Care and Control signed a historic agreement on April 1, 1994, that guarantees a good, loving home to every adoptable cat or dog in San Francisco. The Adoption Pact states that if the Animal Care and Control Center is unable to find a home for any of its healthy cats or dogs, the SF/SPCA will take the animal and guarantee to place him or her. The pact also enables the SF/SPCA to take sick, injured, traumatized, infant and under-socialized animals from the Animal Care and Control Center, rehabilitate them and find them homes, too, thus saving the lives of thousands of treatable animals every year in the Bay Area.

In the first twelve months following the Adoption Pact signing, no adoptable animal was killed in a San Francisco shelter. That meant that all healthy cats and dogs, even if they were old, blind, deaf, disabled or disfigured, were placed in good homes rather than euthanized. The SF/SPCA is working to ensure that the only animals in San Francisco shelters that will be euthanized will be those that are unable to be rehabilitated and for which euthanasia is the only option. These animals may have painful, incurable illnesses or injuries or display aggressive behaviors that pose a threat to public safety.

The theory behind the Adoption Pact is that more people will surrender their unwanted pets to shelters as opposed to abandoning them in the wild or turning them loose on the streets if they have hope that the pet will be placed in a loving home rather than be euthanized. The SF/SPCA Shelter offers a safe refuge, quality nourishment, extensive medical care and lots of love to every animal in its care. The shelter tests cats for incurable diseases and gives each one a health exam as well as a behavior analysis. The shelter's comprehensive health care program includes free spay/neuter surgery prior to placement, vaccinations, deworming and a thirty-day medical-assistance plan after placement. While in the SF/SPCA Shelter, cats reside in individual apartments where they are socialized and showered with tender loving care. A behaviorist is available to modify an animal's behavior if necessary before placement.

In the Adoption Pact's first year of operation, the Animal Care and Control Center had 1,388 animals that were redeemed by their owners and another 2,138 that were adopted. The center transferred 2,219 to the SF/SPCA, where 23 were redeemed and the remainder were adopted out along with other animals already at the shelter. In the first three years of its existence, the Adoption Pact has saved the lives of over 16,000 animals in the Bay Area. The goal of the program is to save the life of every treatable animal and to place him or her in a loving home. The Adoption Pact is funded solely by donations and relies on no tax dollars for support.

The SF/SPCA runs many programs and services that contribute to the success of the pact, generate support and encourage placement of animals with responsible owners. To make it easier and more convenient for people to adopt animals, the SF/SPCA Shelter is open seven days a week with extended hours of operation. To bring the animals to where the people are, the shelter staff and volunteers take prospective adoptees to shopping malls, neighborhood centers, business districts and community events. People who want to adopt a cat can participate in the Dial-A-Cat program, which provides over-the-phone selection, free home delivery and free in-home consultation to responsible caregivers who are unable to come to the shelter due to limited mobility or advanced age. And so that animals can look their absolute best, the SF/SPCA Grooming College provides beauty makeovers for the shelter animals. Grooming services include trimming; clipper cutting; skin, eye and ear care; brushing; bathing and pedicures.

Volunteers have played and continue to play an integral role in the success of the Adoption Pact. In addition to fostering animals in their own homes and participating in animal-socialization programs that make animals more adoptable, volunteers also act as adoption counselors. The shelter uses about 800 volunteers who help match pets with people and educate prospective pet parents on the responsibilities of pet ownership.

The SF/SPCA runs public-awareness campaigns and advertising promotions to spread the word about the animals available for adoption. People are encouraged to adopt and are educated about adoptions via regular Pet of the Week television appearances, public-service announcements on radio and TV, weekly newspaper columns and bus-shelter posters. The SF/SPCA publishes an award-winning magazine, *Our Animals*, about the shelter and SF/SPCA activities.

laughter. Some are so loving and affectionate that they can bring their owners to tears. Some cats are outgoing and love to be the center of attention no matter who or how many people are in the house. Other cats are timid and shy, preferring to hide from strangers and reserving their affection for their owners. Some may be downright skittish and react negatively to loud noises or sudden movements. Others may want to become involved in every single activity in which their owners engage, even when they're running the vacuum cleaner. Some cats exhibit all of these characteristics.

There is no feline personality test that will enable you to predict a cat's personality before you adopt him. Some of the things you should observe with a potential adoption candidate is his or her energy level—and how closely it matches your own. Observe his calmness and how well he may adapt to a bustling household (if you have one), as well as his sense of civility and how well he interacts with other cats (if you have one or other pets). Most important, observe how he responds to you and the sound of your voice when you speak to him. Chapter 4, "Selecting Your Special Cat," will discuss what to look for in terms of a cat's behavior to help you find the right match.

CHAPTER 3

Selecting a Shelter

Virtually everyone in the United States will be able to find a shelter within their geographic region. If you live in a large urban area, you may have several shelters from which to choose. Some shelters are large and have significant financial resources, a paid staff and a large contingent of volunteers. Some are small and operate with little or no paid staff and few volunteers. Regardless of the resources at their disposal, most shelters are run by dedicated people who share a love for animals and want to help them find good homes.

Shelters can be public and not for profit, so they receive tax dollars for their ongoing maintenance and support. Other shelters are private and not for profit and therefore exist on donations and private contributions. Public not-for-profit shelters typically function as the arm of local government and municipalities to conduct animal-control activities, which include picking up animals deemed to be a nuisance or those considered potentially dangerous. Such shelters are often referred to as *the pound* by residents in the region they serve.

Shelters go by many names: SPCA, The Humane Society, Rescue League, and so on. Just because a shelter may carry the name of The Humane Society, however, does not mean that it is affiliated with The Humane Society of the United States. Individual shelters, regardless of what they are called, are generally independent organizations run by people within the communities they serve.

There is no "Good Housekeeping" seal of approval that rates shelters. The American Humane Association has a program that evaluates shelters, their staffing and the programs they offer. Evaluations are at the request of the shelter, at which time the American Humane Association sends a representative to the shelter to perform the process on-site. Evaluations can cost a shelter anywhere from $1,300.00 for a one-day evaluation to $2,500.00 for a two-day evaluation. The final product is a written report that helps the shelter learn what it is doing right and what it could do better, but it is not an approval rating. Shelters are then free to use the information in any way they see fit.

Shelters fall into two other categories as well: those that euthanize pets which have not been adopted within a specified time and those that do not. Shelters that do not euthanize the animals that come to them are called *no-kill* shelters. No-kill shelters are viewed as more humane by the majority of pet owners. Unfortunately, most no-kill shelters, like their counterparts that euthanize pets, have limited space to take in animals and limited financial resources. People wishing to dispose of a family pet, a rescued stray or feral animals are often faced with being placed on waiting lists and must keep the animals themselves until space opens up. Some no-kill shelters, such as the Helen Opperman Krause Animal Foundation, Inc., in Pennsylvania, will not take pets at all, limiting their intake to stray or feral cats and dogs, those whose owners have died or been placed in nursing homes and those who were adopted and returned for whatever reason.

Limited space and limited financial resources to care for the vast number of cats that come to shelters every year means that the overflow will go to shelters that are forced to euthanize cats that can't be placed. The Humane Society of the United States estimates that 30 to 60 percent of all animals brought to shelters are euthanized because there aren't enough homes for them. Although shelters that euthanize perform a service for their respective communities, they often take a bum rap because they must dispose of the majority of animals they take in. Being able to stop cases of euthanasia for treatable and rehabilitatable animals is a goal that humane organizations should work toward nationwide. This problem highlights the importance of programs like the SF/SPCA's Adoption Pact that was discussed in Chapter 2, "What Kind of Cat Do You Want?"

Two or three decades ago, the methods of euthanizing animals were cruel, but today, most shelters provide some type of euthanasia that is quick and painless. As difficult as it is to understand or accept emotionally, shelters that must euthanize animals will continue to

Cats enjoy free roam of the adoption playroom at Tree House Animal Foundation. (Photo courtesy of Tree House Animal Foundation, Inc.)

be in business until pet owners learn to take full responsibility for their adopted animals' entire lifetime and have their pets spayed or neutered.

Among no-kill shelters, there are those that keep cats in individual cages and those that do not. Shelters that keep cats in group or community settings are called *cageless* shelters. In a cageless shelter, cats will be allowed to roam freely in an open area or large room within the shelter. They will be allowed to socialize with other cats known to get along in a multi-cat environment. They should have comfortable beds on which to sleep, cat trees to climb and secluded areas where they can get away from it all.

Shelters that keep cats in separate cages typically have them in a private room away from the noise of barking dogs that, by the way, may be just as stressed in an unfamiliar environment as their feline counterparts. Individual cages are large enough to hold a litter box, usually with newspaper filler, and a food and water dish.

There are some positive and negative aspects to each type of shelter. For the prospective pet parent looking for two cats or one to bring into a household that already has a cat, cageless shelters offer an opportunity to see cats interact with other cats in a group setting. The downside to cageless shelters is that, if the shelter does not isolate and test incoming cats for illnesses before they put them into the group, diseases can spread to all the residents. Shelters also must be careful not to enter a cat into the group who is defensive or aggressive. Such a cat could cause undue stress or physical harm to the rest of the group members.

Cats kept in individual cages are safe from any aggressive cats, but confinement in such a small space may cause added stress to a cat that is already stressed by being in an unfamiliar situation. Cats in no-kill shelters are better off emotionally in cageless situations, because they may be there for an extended time. For the short time that cats are kept in euthanizing shelters (from two to ten days), a separate cage is just fine.

If euthanasia is of concern to you, find out if a shelter keeps its animals until they are adopted or if it euthanizes those that are not adopted into good homes within a certain time. Placing telephone calls to shelters prior to visiting them in person will help you screen out those with philosophies different from your own or those that don't provide the kinds of services discussed later in this chapter that may help you in the long run to keep and care for your cat.

OTHER TYPES OF ADOPTION AVENUES

If you have difficulty locating the kind of cat you want or getting to an animal shelter, you have other options. In addition to the various types of shelters discussed earlier in this chapter, there are some specialty agencies that offer additional places for you to go to find that special cat meant just for you. You may be able to find such agencies listed in the Yellow Pages of your telephone directory under "Animal Shelters" or "Animal Organizations."

ADOPTION AGENCIES

Pet-adoption agencies provide foster homes for cats but have no shelter per se to visit. If there is an overflow of animals, they are boarded with

PROFILE:
ADOPTING A FRIEND FROM FOUR FOOTED FRIENDS

When pet lovers in the Indiana, Pennsylvania, area want to adopt a pet, they can call Four Footed Friends, a local not-for-profit organization that rescues, rehabilitates and adopts out animals in need. Often, the animals that come in are injured from accidents with cars or are dying from dehydration or life-threatening diseases. Accident survivors go to their kennels for treatment and recuperation. Sometimes, they are strays trapped by area residents.

"As a rule, we do not take owned pets unless the owner has died," says Sharon Steigman, president of the board of directors. "Instead we advise the owner how to find a good home for their pet or inform them of other options."

A local newspaper advertises, at no cost to the organization, a listing of the pets available for adoption in its Classifieds section. The group also works with other area shelters to share information about what animals they have for adoption. It also has a listing in the Yellow Pages of the local telephone book under the heading "Animal Shelters." Four Footed Friends goes to the regional shopping malls with educational displays containing photos of the pets available. Local pet stores display photos of pets at the Four Footed Friends kennels where the animals reside. When people see the listings, they call or stop by the kennels.

Four Footed Friends is run solely by volunteers and handles about 200 animals a year. In addition to providing veterinary care, it provides ongoing shelter for the animals until they are adopted into good homes. It also provides a computerized lost-and-found service for pets with Four Footed Friends tags. This organization is funded entirely from donations from supporters in its community.

a participating veterinarian or boarding kennel. A local shelter will know if such an agency exists in your area and what kind of reputation it has. If you would like to find out what cats an adoption agency has available, call its hot line, leave a message and someone will get back to you. Spay/neuter organizations often provide this type of service in addition to their low-cost spay and neuter surgeries.

OUTREACH SERVICES

Getting the animals to where the people are, and therefore making it easier to adopt them, is a goal of many shelters across the country. Not everyone has easy access to a shelter or, due to physical limitations or time constraints conflicting with shelter hours of operation, they can't make it to the nearest shelter. To help get their animals to the potential pet parents, many shelters conduct outreach services within the communities they serve.

Outreach involves taking selected pets to area places of business, setting up a localized adoption service where those interested in adopting an animal can see which ones are available and placing the pet the same day. People wanting to adopt at an outreach event must go through the same kind of stringent screening as they would if they had come to the animal shelter directly.

PROFILE:
ON THE ROAD IN DENVER

In order to make its services more accessible to the community, the Denver Dumb Friends League (DDFL) of Denver, Colorado, instituted several outreach programs that enable it to take its animals and its message to events throughout the region it serves.

The Offsite Outreach program makes in excess of 250 community visits per year to festivals, shopping malls and expos, including the Colorado Home and Garden Expo, the Business to Business Expo, the Garden Show and the Rocky Mountain Pet Expo. In addition to placing more than 150 pets in new

The Denver Dumb Friends League brings pets and educational services to the community. (Photo by Lani Kian, courtesy of Denver Dumb Friends League.)

homes at these events, the two full-time outreach specialists and the volunteers accompanying them are able to offer pet-care tips, discuss responsible pet ownership and share information about the league with more than 200,000 residents.

During the summer months, the league regularly visits King Soopers stores through a partnership with Kal Kan™ pet foods. On each visit, the temperature-controlled Careavan carries six or seven adoptable pets, along with one of the DDFL's outreach specialists who is available to answer questions about the Denver Dumb Friends League and pet care and ownership. Although the Careavan functions as an off-site adoption service, its main goal is education.

The Denver Dumb Friends League was founded in 1910. It is a private, not-for-profit animal-welfare organization that shelters more than 21,000 lost, unwanted and abandoned animals each year. The league has a staff of about 105 employees and more than 325 volunteers who actively strive to find homes for their animals.

HOLISTIC SHELTERS

Some shelters provide their cats with specific kinds of care, such as holistic veterinary medicine and nutrition. They typically will vaccinate their cats according to the laws of the state in which they are incorporated, but they treat their animals when necessary with herbal medicine, homeopathy, acupuncture or a variety of other holistic methods. Such shelters also provide allopathic treatments, such as surgeries, if necessary.

PROFILE:
HOMEOPATHIC CAT CARE

Ember was a ten- to twelve-year-old black cat that was brought to the North Country Animal League (NCAL), a holistic shelter in Vermont, as a stray. He was missing a hind leg, and blood tests showed that he was in renal failure. A homeopathic veterinarian prescribed a remedy for him, and the staff put him on a special homemade diet designed to help cats suffering from kidney failure. Although the staff members were saddened at first, fearing that they could not help Ember, the care given to him turned his life around. Ember became an active cat who once again enjoyed life. Diet and homeopathic remedies helped Ember when conventional medicine might have given up.

The NCAL was founded in 1994 by Jan Gordon Stangel, its executive director, who was a volunteer at a local boarding facility at the time. Because she was dissatisfied with the care of these animals, she decided to found the NCAL, a not-for-profit shelter dedicated to providing more humane care for and treatment of animals. The shelter, originally called The Lamoille County Humane Society, changed its name to the North Country Animal League in 1996.

The NCAL's philosophy is that because animals are part of the environment, the relationship between people and animals is special and that, because people have chosen to domesticate animals, they have a moral responsibility to care for them. The organization uses a holistic approach to animal care, including high-quality foods that are often supplemented with home-prepared meals of grains, vegetables, vitamins and oils. Cats are handled at least once a day.

Animals needing health care are seen by a homeopathic veterinarian. Homeopathy was developed in Germany in the 1800s and draws on the body's own tendency to heal itself. (For more information on holistic health care and homeopathy, see Chapter 6, "Cat Care Basics.") If the animal needs surgery, it is taken to an allopathic veterinarian.

NCAL's mission is to promote animal welfare by offering shelter to the community's orphaned, abused and abandoned animals; providing humane education; fostering humanity and gentleness toward animals; encouraging responsible pet care; investigating cruelty allegations and engaging in a therapy program for elderly pets.

CYBERSPACE ADOPTION

Pet lovers who are hooked up to the Internet and World Wide Web will find many shelters and other cat organizations listed there. Many profile the animals they currently have up for adoption, so browsing the Web may be a way for the digitally inclined to start looking for a special cat.

Cat lovers participating in FELINE-L, the Internet listserv for people who want to communicate with other cat lovers about cats and their care, also can become a member of the Feline Underground Railroad (FUR), which takes rescued cats and shuffles them across whatever area is necessary to ultimately place them in good homes. See Chapter 10, "Resources," for more information on how to locate a cat that's right for you.

PET SHOP CO-OPS

The whole is greater than the sum of its parts. So the saying goes when people describe the benefits of teamwork. When individuals band together to accomplish a particular goal, they have a greater chance of succeeding. To increase the number of outlets from which they can place pets, shelters and pet shops have begun to band together to increase their chances of reaching people who want to adopt a cat or a dog. Pet store and animal shelter cooperation creates a win-win situation for both participants.

When pet shops opt to function as off-site adoption agencies for humane societies and animal shelters, they continue to provide a service for their customers who enjoy seeing the pets in their stores without contributing to the cycle of puppy- or kitten-mill animal production that causes thousands of animals to suffer every year. Shelters essentially obtain a secondary adoption agency with staff they do not have to hire to perform the task. By working closely with the pet shop, the shelter can make sure that store personnel follow the same adoption guidelines that the shelter does.

In such arrangements, pet-store owners consider having the animals in the store for their customers to be a service as well as a marketing tool to get people into the store. As a result, adoption fees generally go directly to the animal shelter.

SPECIAL PROGRAMS AND SERVICES

Good shelters offer special programs that help make their cats more adoptable. How many programs a shelter can offer depends on its financial resources, its staff and volunteer contingent and the creativity and drive of its management. Often, shelter resources are so taxed simply by caring for the influx of animals that very little time and energy remains to do more in the way of fund-raising, legislative lobbying and developing special programs.

Shelters typically have a core staffing contingent that may include a manager or executive director, office personnel to receive and adopt out animals and, if they are fortunate, an animal-cruelty investigator who operates under the laws of the municipality served by the shelter. Larger shelters may have staff members who perform many other functions, such as managing the office, running grooming facilities, working on behavior modification and consulting, recruiting and coordinating the work of volunteers. To do a great deal of the other work associated with running a shelter, they rely heavily on volunteers who perform a number of tasks, including operating many of the special programs they offer. You'll learn more about how shelters use volunteers in Chapter 9, "In Service to Others."

Socialization

Socializing cats, especially those that were once stray or feral cats, is a method used by shelters such as the Tree House Animal Foundation, the San Francisco SPCA and Animal Friends, Inc., to accustom the cats to being handled by humans. Many of the cats that find their way into shelters have had little or no contact with people or have had only negative contact. If they were mistreated, neglected or victims of outright cruelty, they will need some degree of rehabilitation to make them trusting again.

Some programs are informal. Staff members and volunteers come to the shelters, play with the animals, and pet and groom them whenever they are able. Human contact lessens the stress felt by the animals and makes them more social. Other programs are more structured. In such programs, all cats in the shelter are required to be handled for a certain amount of time or are allowed a specified time to be out of their cages each day. They may be housed in certain areas of the shelter to allow them to overcome whatever difficulties they may have prior to being placed for adoption.

Still other programs involve not just getting the cats accustomed to being handled but also modifying any inappropriate behavior that decreases the animal's chances of being adopted. On-staff behavior consultants work with trained volunteers to help decrease a cat's aggressive tendencies, for example, and make her less of a biter. Or, they may turn a shy, skittish cat into one that loves being on a person's lap.

Whatever the reason or nature of a shelter's program, socializing benefits not only the animals but also the future pet owners. Those who work toward socializing animals are a great source of information about a particular pet's personality.

Fostering

Many shelters, such as Animal Friends, Inc., The Humane Society of Huron Valley in Ann Arbor, Michigan, and the Helen Opperman Krause Animal Fund, Inc., run foster-care programs to help rehabilitate kittens and cats and make them more appealing to prospective pet parents. Foster-care programs are run by shelter volunteers who offer feral, injured or sick animals temporary homes where they are socialized and provided with any necessary medical care, including any vaccinations required for young kittens. Fostering cats is a labor of love, and most often, these foster-pet parents bear the financial burden of the temporary care without reimbursement from the sponsoring shelter.

The goal of foster-care programs is to rehabilitate cats that the shelter staff feels will have a chance for adoption—not to simply find additional cage space with shelter volunteers. If the foster program is a good one, the shelter will require that volunteers operate under specific guidelines, including following procedures such as accepting only the cats the shelter staff feels should be fostered and returning the foster pets to the shelter when they are ready to go to a permanent home instead of acting as a secondary adoption agency.

Both socializing and fostering will enable you to find out more about cats that interest you; you'll also be able to talk to the shelter staff members and volunteers, who will have additional information about specific cats that have benefited from the programs.

PROFILE:
BABY BOOM HITS THE SAN FRANCISCO SPCA

In the summer of 1994, shortly after signing its historic Adoption Pact with the San Francisco Animal Care and Control Department, the San Francisco SPCA was hit with an influx of newborn kittens and puppies. The organization was prompted to launch a massive effort to recruit additional foster parents to care for the newborns and their mothers until it was safe to adopt them out to permanent homes.

Several local radio and television stations aired appeals, and ads ran in Bay Area newspapers. Notices were posted in area pet shops, veterinarian waiting rooms, law offices, Laundromats and libraries. During the month of July 1994, when the influx of newborns stretched the SF/SPCA's resources to the breaking point, over 130 new volunteer "angels for animals" called to help.

A local waitress who loved cats passed out flyers along with servings and took two kittens to foster. A bank vice president sent out the appeal in the bank's interbranch mail to over 1,000 branch banks in the Bay Area. The result was one of the most successful recruitment campaigns for the SF/SPCA.

The SF/SPCA's foster pet parent program began in 1978 and currently uses over 600 volunteers who provide extra-tender loving care to more than 1,550 newborn strays and homeless adult pets each year, helping to ensure that they find special homes of their own. The SF/SPCA provides volunteers with food, medication, if needed, and information about how to care for the felines in their charge.

An SF/SPCA foster parent provides nourishment to a motherless kitten. (Photo courtesy of the San Francisco SPCA.)

Medical Care

The kind of medical attention shelters can offer their residents varies considerably. Larger shelters with greater financial resources will have

Sick cats at the Helen Opperman Krause Animal Foundation, Inc., stay in a hospital ward until they are well enough to be adopted into loving homes. (Photo courtesy of Karen Commings.)

veterinarians on staff who treat animals that need medical attention—whether it is when the animal first arrives or on an ongoing basis.

If the shelter does not have veterinarians on staff, it may have a cooperative arrangement with a veterinarian in private practice who treats the shelter animals when necessary. Some shelters use trained veterinary technicians who can give cats medication, administer shots and vaccinations and provide animals with other types of medical attention when it is needed. The technicians may be paid staff or volunteers. When you are shopping for a shelter, don't assume that just because a shelter has no on-staff veterinarian it will not provide good medical care for the animals.

No-kill shelters are the most likely shelters to spay and neuter animals before they are adopted. For shelters that expect to keep an animal for only a few days to a week before it will be euthanized, performing this surgery represents an unnecessary expense. Even if the shelter is not spaying and neutering its animals, it should be working with local veterinarians or spay/neuter agencies to ensure that the surgery occurs for all animals the shelter adopts out. The importance of this operation to help prevent the pet-population problem can't be overemphasized. You'll learn more about the importance of spaying and neutering in Chapter 6, "Cat Care Basics," but if the shelter has not performed this necessary surgery before you take your cat home, it will require you to have it done when the cat is of age if it is a truly responsible facility.

Not every shelter has the resources to test cats for life-threatening illnesses. As with spaying and neutering, testing for contagious diseases is typically performed by no-kill shelters and those that house their animals in communal areas. In such instances, testing the animals and then keeping separate any animals that receive positive test results keeps the diseases from spreading.

If you are adopting a cat to bring into a household that already has a healthy resident cat, you should keep the new cat separate until you can have her tested by your veterinarian. If knowing beforehand whether a cat has been tested for life-threatening conditions is important to you, inquire whether the shelter conducts such tests when you make your preliminary phone call.

Pet-Care Information

When you adopt a cat from a shelter, expect to be given a cat-care kit that includes useful information for the first-time cat owner. Your kit may include some samples of cat food. It also may include coupons for food and litter products, lists of cat-care books at your local library and general member and policy information about the shelter where you adopted your cat.

Shelters often work with pet-food manufacturers to obtain the cat-care booklets and food samples. Such partnerships work for both parties. The shelters are able to reduce their costs, and the pet-food manufacturers benefit by advertising their products to new pet owners.

The information given to you by a shelter will get you started on your way to providing quality care to your new cat but probably won't offer the details you will need as you and your cat grow together. Visit your local library or bookstore and browse the collection of cat books. Buying a comprehensive cat-care book will enable you to have information readily available, but borrowing a book from the library is free, and you can borrow as many as you like and as often as you need them.

There are several excellent magazines on the market that will help you keep abreast of the latest in cat care. Check Chapter 10, "Resources," for a list of these magazines as well as some recommended cat-care books for you to read.

ADOPTION POLICIES

To some, adopting a cat from a shelter may seem as difficult as adopting a baby. Shelters routinely screen potential adopters to help ensure that their cats find good homes with people who are going to be committed to their care, take an active interest in the animals and not dispose of them if and when they become inconvenient.

Such screening is necessary to determine that the cat will be adopted into a good home and serves to educate the new pet owner about proper care of the animal. Once you have brought your cat home, expect to be called within a week or two by the shelter to see how you and your cat are managing. If you would like to know beforehand what kinds of questions to expect, see the profile of the Helen Opperman Krause Animal Foundation pet-placement interview at the end of Chapter 4, "Selecting Your Special Cat."

FEES

Although you will not purchase a cat at a shelter in the way you might at a pet store, don't expect to go to a shelter to get a "free" cat. As was discussed in Chapter 1, "So, You Want to Adopt a Cat," all shelters require some type of monetary contribution at the time of adoption, and contributions vary from shelter to shelter. Adoption fees cover the costs of caring for the cats at the shelter and overhead costs such as medical care, staffing and maintaining the physical building that houses the animals. Some shelters may receive local tax funds, but many do not, so your adoption fee and donation will help contribute to the ongoing costs of running the shelter.

To help as many people as possible who want to adopt pets but may be limited by financial constraints, many shelters offer special prices to those who qualify, such as

Adopt One Cat

get a second cat or kitten
(of lesser adoption fee)
for $10.00!

Pay Spay/Neuter
Deposit
on youngest cat
ONLY!

The Humane Society of Harrisburg Area offers discounts to prospective pet owners who want to adopt two cats at the same time. (Poster courtesy of the Humane Society of Harrisburg Area.)

seniors on a fixed income or those with disabilities who may have limited employment opportunities.

In addition to an adoption fee, shelters may require you to pay for a spay or neuter operation at the time of adoption, so ask what other costs you might incur when the time comes for you to shop for your cat companion.

Once you adopt your cat, you may want to continue to help the shelter where you adopted her by becoming a member. Shelter memberships involve paying an annual fee—usually in the $15.00-to-$25.00 range. This entitles you to additional services, such as receiving a newsletter and gaining admittance to special events and membership meetings.

AFTER THE ADOPTION

Many shelters offer ongoing services for people who have adopted animals from them. If the shelter has a veterinary clinic on the premises or next to the shelter, adoptive parents may have the option to use their services—sometimes at a lower rate than they might find elsewhere. The shelter may offer free medical services—such as insulin if the animal is diabetic. When you make your preliminary phone calls to shelters in your area, ask what services they offer. Finding this out may tell you how committed they are to helping you with the continued care of your cat.

PROFILE:
SHARING LOVE, HOPE AND CARING

Fourteen years ago, Lois received Tiger as a gift from her son. A year later, she adopted Tassy, a friend for her cat, from The Marin Humane Society in Novato, California. Lois considers these two cats as precious members of her family. Arthritis, however, keeps Lois from performing some of her cat-care duties, but not the ones that require her to hold and love her favorite felines. To help Lois, a volunteer with The Marin Humane Society's SHARE program visits the house every weekend to clean the litter box, check on the cats' well-being and take the cats to the veterinarian whenever necessary.

Special Human-Animal Relationships (SHARE) is a multi-faceted program that helps people and their companion animals. Its services help those who love and respect animals maintain a special bond with their pets by providing pet-care assistance to low-income seniors and people with disabilities; bringing pets to visit people in facilities where they can no longer have pets, such as hospitals and nursing homes; conducting adoptions for homebound individuals; and collecting pet food and distributing it to people who qualify for their financial assistance. SHARE also offers dog-obedience classes for seniors and their canine companions.

SHARE's Side-by-Side program also provides financial support and volunteer efforts, such as those that help Lois, Tiger

Fifteen-year-old Tassy was adopted by her owner as a companion to Tiger from The Marin Humane Society and also benefits from SHARE's assistance. (Photo courtesy of The Marin Humane Society.)

Fourteen-year-old Tiger and his owner benefit from the continued efforts of The Marin Humane Society's SHARE program. (Photo courtesy of The Marin Humane Society.)

and Tassy, and donates services to pet owners who qualify. SHARE offers assistance in the form of donated pet food, veterinary care, grooming, regular visits to clients, transportation to a veterinarian or groomer, maintenance of litter boxes and emergency boarding of pets in the event of a client's hospitalization. The Marin Humane Society has more than forty-five volunteers working in the Side-by-Side program.

For people who are recuperating from surgery, are permanently disabled and unable to get to a store for pet food or are on a limited budget, SHARE offers Pet Meals on Wheels to help people feed their pets and continue to share their lives with them. Pet Meals on Wheels collects donated pet food from collection boxes placed in pet stores and supermarkets and distributes it to clients of its program. The donations are monitored and collected by The Marin Humane Society volunteers and distributed throughout the county. The society has made arrangements with the Meals on Wheels component of the County Senior Council to deliver food to both people and their pets so that both will receive nutritious meals at the same time.

Those clients who do not receive regular Meals on Wheels receive scheduled deliveries from The Marin Humane Society.

To bring pets to people who are unable to have them, SHARE operates the Animal Assisted Therapy program, which makes regular visits to more than three dozen institutions in Marin County. Patients living in residential facilities, convalescent homes, senior day-care centers, hospitals and their own homes have the opportunity to experience some of the many benefits that companion animals provide without having to worry about the responsibilities associated with owning an animal.

To make it easier for people over the age of sixty-five to adopt a companion animal, SHARE offers them free adoptions and other services. The society is open six days a week, with some extended hours of service. County residents who are homebound are visited by SHARE volunteers who conduct an in-home, pre-adoption interview. When a good match is found, SHARE brings the pet to the person.

In 1989, SHARE was honored nationally when it received the Delta Society's Model Program Award.

The Marin Humane Society was founded in 1907. It offers a wide variety of services that include an animal behavior hot line, a low-cost spay and neuter clinic, summer camps, adult-education programs, puppy- and dog-training classes and an animal-assisted therapy program for seniors and people with AIDS. The Marin Humane Society shelters more than 8,000 animals every year.

CHAPTER 4

Selecting Your Special Cat

Once you begin shopping for your special cat, you will meet a lot of wonderful and interesting felines. It will be obvious to you immediately that almost all of them would love to have you take them home with you. As much as you might want to do so, you will need to narrow your choice to one or perhaps two felines that will be a good fit with you, your lifestyle, your personality and your temperament.

No matter how scientific and logical you are about selecting the right cat, selecting a cat sometimes comes down to the cat choosing you. You may seem to have no control over the choice at all. Maybe a cat responds to the sound of your voice. Perhaps one has that special look in his eyes that makes you feel that he knows you instantly and you him. A cat may have a comical look on his face or markings that make you smile when you look at him. Whatever the reason, bonding with a cat can occur in just a few minutes—almost instantly—after the two of you meet. The right cat for you will have a lot to do with what clicks emotionally at the moment. Despite the magical quality of *love at first sight*, there are a few things you should keep in mind when you begin to shop for Mr. or Ms. Wonderful.

Although a cat initially may seem like the one meant just for you, spend some time learning about him before you decide. (Photo courtesy of Karen Commings.)

Before you begin shopping, you should plan how you will bring home your cat once you've selected him or her. It is extremely dangerous for both you and your cat to have him running freely in your automobile. Your cat may panic and climb on the dashboard, into your steering wheel or under your feet as you try to press the gas or brake peddle. A free-roaming cat won't have the protection of a seat belt, and if you must stop suddenly, your cat could be thrown against a hard surface inside your car and be seriously injured. If you open a door or window, your cat could escape, never to be found again.

Most shelters will insist that you place your adopted cat in a cat carrier. If you do not have one, the shelter will be able to sell you at a minimal cost (roughly $5.00) a cardboard carrier with holes in it so your cat will get air as he rides securely in the carrier.

Such carriers are convenient initially, but in time you may want to think about purchasing a sturdy carrier with a wire door and side slots so that your cat can look out while he is traveling with you. Carriers cost about $15.00 or more, depending on their size. Some are large enough to house your cat, a litter box and a water bowl. Large carriers are useful if you are taking a long trip. Your cat will be able to take care of bodily functions without you having to stop and let him out of the carrier to use a litter box or get a drink of water. Some carriers have wheels that enable you to pull rather than carry them. Wheeled carriers are excellent for pet owners who have back problems. Shop around for a carrier, too. You can find good ones in discount department stores for less than you might pay in a pet store.

VISITING THE SHELTER

You will learn much about a shelter and its inhabitants once you get there and observe it. Although most people who work in shelters have hearts of gold and mean well, not all have the organizational skills to operate the shelter efficiently.

Your first impression may mean a lot in terms of whether the shelter affects you positively or negatively. Does the shelter look clean and sanitary, or are animals forced to lay in dirt? Shelters have staff members or volunteers who regularly clean animal areas and individual cages. Bear in mind that cats may need to relieve themselves periodically throughout the day, so a bit of waste in their litter boxes does not constitute dirty surroundings. The litter boxes and cages should indicate that someone has cleaned them at least once during the day. Under no circumstances should animals be forced to lay in their own waste.

Regardless of whether a shelter uses individual cages or is a cageless shelter, sick animals should be separated from those that are healthy. If cats that are suffering visibly from upper-respiratory diseases are housed with other cats, any cat you select may have contracted the same condition. Respiratory problems are relatively easy to cure, but you must remember that in such a case, you will be making trips to the veterinarian for more than just a checkup relatively soon after bringing your new cat home; you'll find yourself learning about the fine art of feline pill popping before you've learned what kind of treats your cat likes.

Talk to shelter staff members to learn which tests a cat has had. Some shelters have a return policy if a cat adopted from them turns out to have *feline leukemia virus* (FeLV) or *feline immunodeficiency virus* (FIV). As in life, there are no guarantees that a healthy cat will remain healthy forever, but some upfront information from the shelter will help you evaluate your cat's present and future health. Even cats with life-threatening diseases can live happily for many years before symptoms show up. If your new cat tests positive for any such condition, discuss with your veterinarian how to provide the best care under the circumstances.

Shelters should provide cats with healthy, nutritious food daily. Food remaining in the cats' bowls should not look like it has been there for any length of time. Remnants of the day's meals should not be scattered

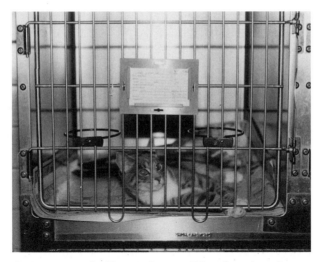

Cats in cages at the Humane Society of Harrisburg Area sleep on warm newspapers. (Photo courtesy of Karen Commings.)

over the shelter floor or an individual cat's cage. Cats should be provided with fresh water in clean bowls at all times.

Cats should also be provided with warm, comfortable places to sleep. If cats are kept in cages, they should not be forced to lie down on wire cage surfaces or mesh but should have a solid surface on which to sleep. Shelters typically provide newspapers, blankets or towels to caged cats to help keep them warm, comfortable and off the metal cage bottom.

YOU'D BETTER SHOP AROUND

All shelters are not the same—despite their good intentions. If staff members do not seem interested in matching you up with the right animal or don't offer much assistance when you ask questions, go elsewhere. Although staff members undoubtedly see too much of the pet-owning public relinquishing their animals again and again, they shouldn't take it out on you. Staff members should be courteous, friendly and willing to talk to you about any cat you see that interests you. By helping you select the right animal, they've taken a step toward ensuring that you won't return him later.

Don't feel pressured into selecting a cat at the first shelter you visit. You are looking for a companion—one you will share your life and home with for a long time to come. Your cat companion will sense as much about how you feel, day in and day out, as any human friend. Your cat will be there to console you when you are feeling down, amuse you when you want to have fun, relax with you when you've had a hard day or just be there, sharing whatever activities occupy your time. So, choosing the right cat is an important decision.

You may have to visit several shelters or even the same shelter several times before you find the cat that is right for you. There is a high turnover of animals in shelters. Shelters that are forced to euthanize their animals may offer cats for only two to four days (depending on cage availability) before they are adopted or put to sleep. When you revisit a shelter after a week or so, you may find an entirely different contingent of cats from which to choose.

Please don't feel that you must take a cat simply to save him from being euthanized. The clearer and more focused you can be about the kind of cat for which you want to provide a good, permanent home, the more you will contribute to preventing the countless unnecessary deaths of cats that occur every year. Every little bit helps, and by providing a good home to even one feline that you will care for his entire lifetime, you will be taking a step in the direction of preventing euthanasia everywhere.

TIMING IS EVERYTHING

When you visit a shelter, choose a time when you feel relaxed and unhurried. Selecting the perfect pet should be fun, not just something to check off on your to-do list. Don't shop for your special cat on a day when you have a half dozen other things you must accomplish and can give the selection only part of your time and concentration. You don't want to drag a cat around with you when you go to the dry cleaner or stop for groceries, and you don't want to have to get to know your new cat companion when you have to rush home to fix dinner.

Don't visit a shelter at an inappropriate time of the year, such as before a holiday, a significant event or a vacation. Emotional times or events may cause you to make poor choices.

In order to select the right cat, you will want to spend time with many of the animals you meet. You must keep your mind clear and your heart open to meeting the right cat at any moment. You might find the perfect feline on your first day out, but you might not. Choosing a cat that will spend his entire life with you is certainly more important than finding an outfit for that special party or important meeting. You wouldn't want to buy something that doesn't fit, so don't hurry to choose a cat that might not fit your temperament or your lifestyle.

SNAPSHOT:
Giorgio

When pet lover Essie Newman went with a friend to the East Shore Shelter of the Humane Society of Harrisburg Area, she intended to help her friend select a pet. The friend was adopting a cat for the first time and didn't know how to pick one, so Newman had offered to help her make an appropriate selection.

"The hardest thing is narrowing it down to one," says Newman. "It's not easy walking out of there seeing all of their little faces."

While making the rounds of the cages, Newman saw a little black-and-white cat named Griffin. "I felt sorry for him, because he was a return," Newman says. "He was so cute I couldn't pass him by."

Newman had recently lost her one-year-old tuxedo cat, Corky, to complications due to feline urinary tract disease and thought that another tuxedo might help her overcome the loss. She took ten-week-old Griffin out of his cage to see how he responded to her, if he enjoyed being held and petted and how much love he showed.

"He couldn't have cared less that I was there," says Newman. "He just wanted to play, but he was so adorable that I took him anyway. He turned out to be a real sweetheart."

That evening, a cat named Cleo went home with Newman's friend, and Griffin came home with Newman to a household that included four other cats. Newman changed Griffin's name to Cory and then to Giorgio, after the perfume, presumably because of his sophisticated appearance and his sweet disposition. Giorgio had no trouble learning his new name.

Over the years, Giorgio has developed into what Newman calls "the nicest cat." "Everyone goes nuts over him," she says.

Giorgio peeks out from under a table covering at the Newman household. (Photo courtesy of Essie Newman.)

BE PREPARED

Take a pencil and paper with you and make notes about cats that interest you or about the shelter itself. If you are visiting several shelters or large shelters, you will see lots of animals, and remembering each cat and each shelter may be difficult unless you write down your thoughts.

Talk to staff members and volunteers about cats that interest you. Don't be afraid to ask questions about any cat. The staff and volunteers may be able to tell you about the cat's history and his behavior since coming to the shelter. Add any information they give you to your notes.

When cats are brought to some shelters, the person relinquishing the animal must fill out an intake form, or spec sheet, that lists information about the animal's background. How did the person acquire the animal? Did he live indoors or outdoors? Does he get along with men, women and children? In addition to the answers to these questions, shelter staff members will make comments and provide information that will be beneficial to the pet's new owner, such as when the cat was vaccinated, spayed or neutered and treated medically (if ever).

PROFILE:
KITTY SPEC SHEETS

The staff at Animal Friends, Inc., requires that every person who brings in an animal fill out an intake form that provides prospective pet parents with extensive information about the animal, where it came from, how it behaved and why it was being placed up for adoption.

You may question whether a person relinquishing an animal would offer accurate information. When people bring animals to no-kill shelters where they know pets will not be euthanized, though, they will likely be truthful about the pet's personality or any behavioral problems. A sample intake form follows. Feel free to make copies of this form and take it with you to use as a means of collecting information about your potential new cat. Compare it with intake forms the previous cat owners filled out and fill in any missing information by asking the staff or volunteers.

Sample Intake Form or Worksheet

What is the cat's name, sex and age?

_____

What is the cat's color and markings?

_____

What is the cat's weight? Has it been spayed or neutered? If so, when? Has it been declawed?

_____

What are the dates of the cat's last inoculations, and what were they?

_____

Has the cat had any serious illnesses or injuries?

_____

What was the age of the cat when the owner acquired it?

_____

What were the ages of the children in the household when the cat lived there?

_____

What other pets were in the household?

_____

How was the cat disciplined?
_____

Check if the cat responds to these words:
❏ No! ❏ Come ❏ Its name

Check if the cat has displayed any of the following characteristics:
❏ Urinating outside the litter box
❏ Defecating outside the litter box
❏ Crying excessively
❏ Jumping or climbing on counters
❏ Clawing furniture
❏ Scratching people
❏ Growling at people
❏ Hissing at people
❏ Biting people
❏ Fighting with dogs
❏ Fighting with cats
❏ Eating houseplants
❏ Catching mice
❏ Using a scratching post

Is the cat 100-percent litter-box trained?
_____

What type of litter was used?
_____

Where was the litter pan kept?
_____

How often was the litter box cleaned?
_____

What was the feeding schedule, cat-food brand and amount given?
_____

What toys will the cat play with?
_____

Will the cat walk on a leash?
_____

Does the cat react negatively to the following:
❏ Men   ❏ Strangers
❏ Women   ❏ Travel
❏ Infants ❏ Being groomed
❏ Toddlers ❏ Being boarded
❏ Children

Why are you giving up the cat?
_____

If a shelter uses spec sheets or intake forms, ask to see them. The forms will give you additional information about the cats. For example, if you have children or lots of visitors, you may want to get a cat known to get along with children or one that will not be afraid of strangers. An intake form may provide you with that information. Add any relevant information to your notes. An intake form also may help you provide your cat with the same kind of care that he is accustomed to, such as the same brand of cat food or cat litter. It also may guide you in deciding that a particular cat is not the right pet for you.

If the shelter has a program that socializes cats, you will learn much about a particular cat by talking to the staff members or volunteers who socialize them. They will be able to provide you with current information about how the animal behaves, his likes and dislikes and how he interacts with humans and other cats.

Many animals that arrive at shelters have come from a life on the street or from the wild and need to spend some time with humans in positive settings before they are ready and able to adapt to lives inside the home. A stray cat or one that has come from a feral environment will make a wonderful pet, given time and patience on your part, however, so you should not be dissuaded from adopting one on that basis alone.

GETTING TO KNOW YOU

When you are visiting with the cats at the shelters, talk to them. Cats that want to meet you will respond to the sound of your voice. Many people feel a little silly talking to an animal, but the sound and tone of your voice is one important method for your cat to get to know you. Cats are sensitive, perceptive creatures capable of feeling a wide range of emotions. They will be able to tell a lot about you when you communicate with them. Shelter cats must compete for attention, too, so hearing the sound of a human voice directed toward them will help them find solace and comfort.

If the cat's name is posted on the cage, address the cat by name. If you end up choosing a cat whose name you don't like, don't worry. A cat, no matter how old, can learn a new name as well as one or more nicknames, so don't feel obligated to keep the cat's first name if another one suits you, or the cat, better.

Communicating with a cat is important in finding one with which you can bond emotionally. (Photo courtesy of Margaret G. Stanley, Animal Friends, Inc.)

Like humans, cats communicate in many ways—through body language, facial expressions and their vocal chords. Cats speak a language of their own that you will come to learn as you live with one. Cats make many different sounds that can mean many things, depending on the cat. Some cats communicate using little chirping sounds that seem to indicate that they are contented or happy. At other times, a cat may communicate using sounds that are loud and forceful. These sounds seem to indicate that a cat wants something from you or wants you to do something like toss one of his toys or open a can of cat food. Sometimes cats put various sounds together in long strings that appear to be the feline equivalent of sentences. Of course, not all cats consider carrying on a conversation with their person to be necessary or even worthy of their time. This type of cat will forever remain the strong, silent type whose communications may be limited to the proverbial arch of the back as he rubs proudly against your legs or the placid smile as he dozes at your side.

One of the most common forms of feline communication is the purr. A cat's purr is one of the most soothing sounds in nature, unduplicated in any other species. Purring is common even among the big wildcats.

Cats purr when they are happy, but they also purr when they are nervous, when they are in pain and, yes, even when they are dying. No one

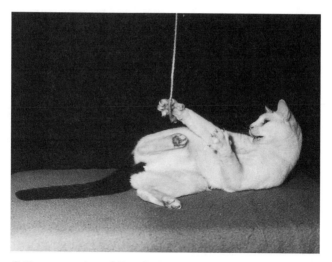

C.C., a cat at Animal Friends, Inc., enjoys playing a game. (Photo courtesy of Margaret G. Stanley, Animal Friends, Inc.)

is sure exactly how a cat purrs, but the most recently accepted theory is that purring is caused by the flow of blood through a vein called the *vena cava* in the cat's chest cavity. When the muscles contract around the vein, the resulting vibrations produce an air turbulence that creates the purring sound. Whatever the cause, if you detect a cat purring when you approach his cage or talk to him, you can be sure that he's happy to make your acquaintance.

Pet and stroke the cat and observe how he responds. If he hisses or spits when you attempt to pet him, don't force the issue. If he seems to want to avoid being touched by retreating to the back of the cage, he may have had a negative experience with a human in his past or is simply not accustomed to being petted. Such cats may make wonderful pets but will require a little more time and attention to make them enjoy the human touch. If you are up to the challenge, your cat will repay you handsomely for the rest of his life.

You will be able to tell within a short time whether a cat wants to get to know you. A cat that is interested in knowing you better will appear attentive and alert and may approach you if he is not confined to an individual cage. Even cats in cages will let you know if they are interested in making your acquaintance by sitting or standing up and coming to the front of the cage.

Cats that are not interested or are frightened may retreat from you altogether if they are living in a communal area, may not respond at all if they are in cage or, in some cases, may exhibit threatening body language. A cat that is defensive about being approached may lower or flatten his ears, hiss and spit or swat if you extend your hand to pet him. If a cat is frightened or defensive, his eyes will be wide and the pupils dilated. His appearance is designed to frighten away anyone or anything that is causing him to feel threatened.

Fortunately, unapproachable cats are in the minority, but to be sure, extend your hand slowly to pet a new feline to see how he responds. A cat may rub his face or body against you. Rubbing is a way that cats mark their territory with their scent. That territory can include you as the cat's owner or potential owner. When they wash, cats lick themselves in the direction in which their hair grows. Rubbing their bodies along you or an object is also a sensory action that provides the cat with a pleasurable experience and says that he likes you. If he begins purring, appears to want to play or rubs against you or his shelter cage, you can be sure that he's interested.

To help you get to know more about each of the cats you see at the shelters, take along a cat toy for the animal to play with. An interactive toy that has an appealing item, such as a piece of fabric on the end of a string tied to a pole, is ideal. It will offer you the opportunity to see the cats' energy levels and help you match one to yours. A small, lightweight, rubber ball to roll is another good choice of toy. Both options allow you to play with the cats without risking getting accidentally scratched.

If the shelter houses its cats in a communal environment, you will see cats climbing over one another to play with you and the toy. You will find that the mere notion of playing a game may send them into a frenzy of cat heaven. If cats are kept in individual cages at the shelter you are visiting, take one out at a time to play with. Don't remove more than one at a time, because you don't know how the cats will interact with one another. The last thing you want is for two cats to begin fighting and potentially harm each other. Remember that shelters are a stressful environment for cats, and forcing them to interact with strange cats just compounds their anxiety. If the cats are in communal areas, the shelter staff already has determined that they can coexist in harmony.

PROFILE:
FRIED'S CAT SHELTER

Hans and Lucille Fried fled Nazi Germany in 1939. In the United States, they began caring for all the stray and neglected animals they saw. While they were employed, the Frieds volunteered for a local Humane Society.

Believing strongly that it is just as wrong to kill animals as it is to kill humans, Hans and Lucille Fried sold their home and possessions in 1977 to open a cat shelter. Over time, the shelter has held as many as 900 cats. Inspired by the no-kill policy of Chicago's Tree House Animal Foundation, the Frieds wanted to open a shelter that did not put to death the thousands of animals they saw being euthanized at other shelters. The purpose of Fried's Cat Shelter is to serve as a place of love and hope for the hundreds of deserted and suffering cats and to offer them a safe haven for the rest of their natural lives. Built with the Frieds' life savings in the shell of an old motel, Fried's Cat Shelter in Michigan City, Indiana, has offered safe refuge to homeless and unwanted cats for more than two decades.

In 1988, a tragic fire destroyed the original shelter. Ten of the 500 cats in the shelter were lost, and the building suffered more than $100,000.00 in damages. Thanks to the Frieds and a dedicated group of cat lovers, a new shelter consisting of three separate buildings was constructed. The main building has a hospital, recuperating area and isolation ward for incoming cats. There are separate areas to house kittens and senior cats. A separate building is the quarantine area, and a third building is the feline leukemia sanitarium. Most of the cats stay in a large, open area in the main shelter called the Charlie and His Gang Living Quarters after a resident cat that had complete run of the shelter. The shelter also has a boarding facility called the Feline Hilton Hotel.

Cats coming to Fried's Cat Shelter are examined by a veterinarian, spayed or neutered and then are offered for adoption.

Adoption fees, which are nonrefundable donations, range from $25.00 to $55.00, depending on whether the cat has been neutered and what shots he has had. Adoption fees include a carrier.

Cats not adopted are allowed to live out their lives in total freedom, safe from harm, in the large, cageless main area that houses the animals. Fried's neither cages nor kills, but instead spays and neuters. The only euthanasia that occurs is when a cat is extremely ill, is suffering and cannot be helped. To help defray the ongoing costs of maintaining the shelter and providing a safe haven for the cats, Fried's sells items in its gift shop located in the facility's main office.

Hans Fried died in 1991, and Lucille Fried passed away in 1993 at the age of 96. Fried's Cat Shelter is a private, not-for-profit organization and continues the work of Hans and Lucille.

THE ADOPTION PROCESS

Once you decide on a cat to adopt, you will need to fill out some forms and provide the shelter with information about yourself. At the time of adoption, you also will be required to pay whatever fee the shelter asks to adopt your cat. Find out at that time if you are required to pay any other costs, such as for spaying or neutering. Even if your cat has not been altered, you may have to arrange for the operation at the time of adoption and pay the cost through the shelter. Such arrangements usually mean that you will obtain the surgery at a reduced cost compared to what you would have to pay on your own through your veterinarian. Some pet parents prefer to use their own vets, because they have established a rapport with them and are familiar with them. You may have to discuss this issue with a shelter staff member at the time of adoption.

Shelters have contributed time and effort to make their cats adoptable, so it is not surprising that they want to ensure that their animals get the best homes possible. You will have to fill out a form that asks you for all sorts of information about you and your living situation, how you will care for the cat and what kind of home you will be providing. Don't be offended by any of the questions you are asked. You are adopting a living creature in which the shelter has invested its resources—financial and otherwise. It is only natural for the shelter to want to ensure that the cat's needs continue to be met.

PROFILE:
FINDING GOOD HOMES

Nestled in the mountains of Central Pennsylvania is the Helen Opperman Krause Animal Foundation, Inc. (HOKAFI), a shelter founded in the early 1980s by Helen Opperman Krause, an octogenarian who for more than fifty years took stray cats into her home. As a result of her good nature and open-door policy, her house became a place where area residents took rescued animals and strays or relinquished their unwanted pets because they knew the animals would not be euthanized. Assisted by some local citizens, Helen Krause was able to form a not-for-profit organization that enabled her to continue to perform the animal rescue work that was the foundation of her life.

From the roadway, the unobtrusive structures housing the cats' main living area and the hospital ward are barely recognizable as an animal shelter. Only a tiny sign designates its location. No maps point to its whereabouts. Directions to the shelter are given only to those animal lovers who seriously want to adopt a pet or who have acquired animals, such as strays or pets of a loved one who has passed away or entered a nursing home. No dumping is allowed.

Yet HOKAFI's efforts on behalf of pet care and adoption have grown to be some of the most visible in the region it serves. The shelter is run with no official staff but a corps of 200 dedicated volunteers who find homes for more than 100 cats a month.

HOKAFI is a cageless, no-kill shelter with a maximum capacity of approximately 100 cats in its main shelter area. Its adoption counselors use a multistep procedure to find homes for their animals, most of which are cats. The shelter advertises the animals it has available in local newspapers and the shelter newsletter. Posters with photos are sent to veterinarians' offices throughout the geographic region the shelter serves.

Anyone wanting to adopt can call the shelter's adoption line, at which time a preliminary interview takes place. Candidates are asked if they will keep the pet indoors or outdoors, if they rent or own their residence, if they have other pets, if the pets are neutered, what veterinarian they use and if there are any children in the house.

After the preliminary interview, candidates make an appointment to visit the shelter. At the visit, staff members then try to match them with an appropriate animal that fits their temperament and lifestyle. Staff members observe potential pet parents, ask additional questions and ask them to fill out a form with the following questions:

1. What is your name, address and phone number?

2. Do you own or rent; if you rent, what is your landlord's name?

3. Who is your current employer?

4. Do you have any pets now? If yes, what type and ages?

5. Have you had any pets in the past? If yes, what type and ages? If yes, were they spayed or neutered?

6. Why do you want to adopt a kitten/cat?

    ❏   For breeding
    ❏   For catching mice
    ❏   For companionship

7. Where will you keep the kitten/cat?

    ❏   In the house
    ❏   In the basement
    ❏   Outside
    ❏   In the barn
    ❏   Other (explain)

8. If you adopt a kitten, will you take it to be spayed or neutered when it is of age?

9. What would you do with the cat if you had to move?

10. If a situation arose that no longer allowed you to keep the cat (for example, allergy, divorce), what would you do with it?

11. Does anyone in your household have allergies to cats?

12. What is the name of the veterinarian you plan to use?

13. How often do you think a cat should be examined by a vet?

14. Are you familiar with the vaccinations a cat needs to have?

15. Are you familiar with the rabies law in Pennsylvania?

16. What would you do with this cat if it were to become sick within the next two weeks?

17. How much money would you estimate a cat's vaccination and other medical expenses would cost on the average per year?

18. Do you feel financially capable of providing complete health care to the kitten/cat you're interested in adopting?

19. Are you willing to spend the money for veterinary care?

20. Where did you hear about this animal shelter?

21. Why did you choose this animal shelter?

Once approved, adopters are asked to sign the form stating that they agree to abide by the policies of the shelter, including keeping the cat indoors and returning it to the shelter if, for any reason, they are not able to keep the cat. All cats taken from the

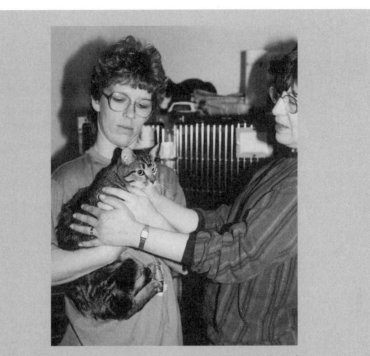

A volunteer at the Helen Opperman Krause Animal Foundation, Inc., helps a prospective pet parent find the right pet. (Photo courtesy of Karen Commings.)

shelter must be placed in a cat carrier. If the adopter does not have one, the shelter has carriers it will sell to the new pet parent.

Following the adoption, pet-placement counselors call the new owner to determine the well-being of the cat. Anyone who has adopted a kitten receives a spay/neuter reminder postcard when the cat is due for the surgery.

HOKAFI is a private, not-for-profit organization that relies on the fund-raising efforts of its volunteers and supporters. In 1995, HOKAFI met its goal to raise money to care for its special-needs residents. Like many of its residents, the shelter was in need of some additional care and space to house the many animals that had arrived. In 1996, its board of directors formed a building-planning committee to review options for a new shelter and began campaigning to raise funds for repairing the building that was once home to Helen Opperman Krause.

CHAPTER 5

Bringing Home Baby

Once you've selected that perfect cat companion, you will embark on the first step of a journey that will be one of the most rewarding experiences of your life—getting to know your cat. The first days you spend with her will be an adventure for both of you. But before you actually bring her home, there are some pre-installation planning activities that require your attention. Being prepared by taking these initial steps will make the learning process a positive one for both of you.

THE BASIC NECESSITIES

We all have those things we just couldn't do without—a place to eat, sleep and take care of daily bodily functions. Your cat has basic needs, too, and as her caregiver, you will need to have certain items available to satisfy those needs when that special day arrives when you bring home your new shelter cat.

In Chapter 1, "So, You Want to Adopt a Cat," you looked at the costs associated with caring for a cat. Now that it's time to buy the basic care items, you might want to invest in items that will last longer instead of ones you will need to replace more frequently. For example, will a larger food bowl, bed or litter pan be adequate for your new kitten and also see him into adulthood? If you think you can accomplish both, buy something that will last and save your extra funds for veterinary care or better quality cat food.

The Bowl

First and foremost are food bowls and water dishes. These come in many shapes, styles and prices. A food bowl should be large enough and wide enough for your cat to lower her face into it without crushing her whiskers against the sides of the bowl. Cats lick their

Most pet stores will have a good supply of nutritious food for your cat. (Photo courtesy of Karen Commings.)

food with their rough tongues, so the sides of the bowl should be curved to prevent food from being licked out onto the floor.

Cat-food bowls can be made of glass, ceramic, metal or plastic material. A word of caution about plastic bowls, however. If your cat is prone to contracting *feline acne* (little black crusty areas on her chin), plastic bowls may exacerbate the condition, because plastic retains the oils in foods.

Some food bowls come with a water bowl attached, but to a cat, eating and drinking aren't related as they are for humans having a meal. Your cat may like to have her water dish somewhere besides right next to her food bowl, so you should obtain two separate bowls rather than a joined one.

If you prefer, you don't need to buy dishes especially for your cat if you have suitable dishes in the house that you can designate as hers. A really useful tip for people who may find their cat's food attracting ants: Sit the bowl of food inside a slightly larger saucer of water. Ants don't swim and will not cross the water to get to your cat's food.

You should have in the house a supply of cat food specifically intended for the nutritional needs of your cat. Kittens should have kitten food, adults should have food intended for the adult cat and seniors should be provided with food for their special needs. You'll learn more about nutrition and premium types of cat food in Chapter 6, "Cat Care Basics," but for your cat's first few days, have a supply of good-quality, commercially available cat food on hand, both wet and dry.

The Box

One of the most important things you will obtain for your cat is a litter box. Litter boxes come in all sizes and shapes, and finding one that suits your cat may take some experimentation. To start, it's best to try a plain box and size it according to the size of your cat. If you have a kitten, a small box is adequate. A larger cat will need a larger box to feel comfortable in it. Once your cat has lived with you for a while, you may want to opt for one of the fancier litter boxes, such as those with hoods that keep litter from being propelled out of them or boxes with inserts that allow you to sift out the waste materials for easy disposal.

At the upper end of the price scale is a relatively new litter box that automatically begins cleaning when the cat steps out of it. The self-cleaning box is timed to start its dirty work ten minutes after Kitty leaves. Such contraptions sell for about $199.00, so you'll have to decide if scooping out the box is so unpleasant that it warrants spending that amount of money. Needless to say, this type of box is designed for the cat owner, not the cat, so your cat will be just as happy with a box that you've cleaned as with one that cleaned itself.

To go with your litter box, you will need a heavy-duty scoop with slots in it so that you can lift out Kitty's waste without disposing of unused litter that comes along with it. There are many types of scoops on the market, and you will do best with one that is about six to eight inches across and has a molded plastic handle that won't break easily.

In addition to the litter box, you will need a supply of cat-box filler. Cat litter comes in many types besides the common clay litter or the newer clumping litter. There are many environmentally safe types of litter as well, made of materials such as wood chips, newspaper pellets and ground corn husks. Some types of litter create more dust than others, so you might want to try different kinds before settling on one that you like. Cats have a wide variety of preferences when it comes to litter, so you may have to do some experimenting to find the type of litter that is suitable for both of you.

Cats have a natural propensity for digging, so getting your cat to use her box simply will require that you show your cat where it is. Placement of the litter box is important, and choosing an inappropriate litter box location is one of the primary reasons why a cat will stop using it. A good litter box spot is one that is convenient for both of you, but to find a place

Cat lovers will find many types and styles of litter boxes from which to choose at local pet stores. (Photo courtesy of Karen Commings.)

that will appeal to a feline, you must start thinking like one. A cat will appreciate a litter box location that is quiet, temperate and private. Yes, cats, too, like privacy in the privy, so putting your cat's box in the garage may discourage her from using it if, every time she does, she is jolted out of it by the garage door going up and a loud automobile coming in. If she must walk past Fido's bed to get to her litter box, she may change her mind about going there and find a more convenient place to perform her bodily functions. The basement may be a great location, as long as the basement door is left open for easy access and the box is not right next to the furnace when it kicks on, especially if it's loud. Cat owners often choose to place the box in the bathroom, laundry room or other out-of-the-way spots that offer comfort for the cat and convenience of cleanup by the owner.

The Bed

Cats are creatures of habit as well as comfort. They will seek out the softest, most comfortable spot to sleep, and because they spend a great deal of time sleeping, they will inevitably find some favorite locations in your home in which to nap. At night, you may find that your cat prefers to be active and play with her favorite toys. Or, you may find her wanting to spend a lot of time looking out the windows. Cats have excellent eyesight, even in the dark, and yours may find lots of nighttime activity outside your windows that you may never see. Moles, mice, rabbits, owls or other wildlife may attract your cat's attention and keep her occupied into the wee hours. Eventually, however, your cat will want to come to bed, and most likely it will be yours.

One of the decisions you will want to make early on is where your cat will sleep. Most cats want to sleep with their owners, but that may not be what you prefer. Or, even if you allow your cat to sleep on your bed, you may want to provide an extra sleeping place just for her. Cat beds come in all styles and shapes, from the sublime to the ridiculous. Some are simply padded cushions or mats. Others are a combination sleeping/playing apparatus that appeals to your cat's need to snuggle and have fun. Still other cat beds match your decor.

Cat beds are priced to suit every pocketbook—from $10.00 or less to as high as $100.00 or more. Your cat, however, won't care how much you paid for the bed. Her major concern will be how comfortable it is, so you may opt for something as basic as a chair cushion that becomes your cat's

Cat beds come in all types and price ranges. (Photo courtesy of Karen Commings.)

regular sleeping place. Just make sure that she knows that the bed or cushion belongs to her by placing her on it. You may want to provide her with several beds or sleeping cushions and place them in cozy corners of your home, such as under your bed or on pieces of furniture, to help keep the cat-hair deposits to a minimum.

The Post

Most cats you adopt from shelters will have their claws intact. Cats scratch for two major reasons. Cats are territorial animals with scent glands on the pads of their feet. Consequently, animal behaviorists believe that cats scratch as a method of marking their territory by depositing their scents on objects. But cats' claws grow rapidly and, by clawing, they remove the old nail sheaths as the new nails grows in.

To protect your furniture from your cat's need to scratch, you will want to supply your cat with a scratching alternative—the cat scratching post. Like beds and litter boxes, manufacturers have developed a wide variety of sizes and styles to appeal to the most discriminating feline tastes. These posts are made from combinations of wood, carpet, *sisal* (a plant with stiff fibers used in rope) or even cardboard. The posts can be freestanding or can hang from doorknobs or bedposts.

Your cat will be drawn to a scratch post naturally. As with the litter box, you just need to show her where it is. A little dry catnip sprinkled on the post will make it more appealing to your cat.

Toys

Playing with your cat is a method of getting to know her. Play also provides exercise, which is so important in keeping your cat healthy and fit and gives her an outlet to practice her hunting skills. Even though you may be keeping your cat indoors, she will retain much of her instinctive behavior, and pouncing on prey is one of them. You will observe over and over your cat playing "cat and mouse" with her playthings.

Toys need not be elaborate or expensive, although there are plenty of those to be found in the marketplace. You can score points with your cat by having a cardboard box or paper grocery sack without handles available for her to run and jump in. Crumpled paper balls are a favorite with cats that like to chase. Just make sure that the toys you give your cat are

Cat lovers will find a wide variety of scratch posts and toys at a pet store. (Photo courtesy of Karen Commings.)

safe. Any toy with small parts or bells should not be given to a cat without first removing those parts that she could pull off and accidentally ingest. If a toy has a string attached to it, allow her to play with it only under your supervision.

If you adopt a kitten, chances are the smell of catnip will not mean much to her until she is older—about eight weeks or more. Some cats never fully appreciate catnip, but having a catnip toy or two on hand when you bring home your adult cat companion might be a pleasant way to say "I love you."

The Brush

Grooming will be an important part of caring for your cat, so investing in a good-quality brush and comb will pay off in the long run. You will be able to keep hairballs and hair deposits to a minimum by daily grooming. You'll look at the importance of good grooming in Chapter 6, "Cat Care Basics," but for now, visit a pet store and pick up a soft-bristled brush and fine-toothed comb. Regular brushing and combing is a way to share quality time with your cat, so starting the process right away will be another way to initiate bonding and accustom her to being handled.

SAVING MONEY

It may seem like you have to spend a lot of money on basic necessities, but there are some cost-saving measures that will help you avoid some initial expenses and enable you to set aside some money for veterinary care or premium-quality food if you prefer to target those items. The following are some techniques that will help you provide the necessary care items for your cat and save money at the same time. Use your imagination to think of more ways you can make your cat's life safe and enjoyable and save money as well.

Pet stores will have a wide variety of grooming tools from which to choose. (Photo courtesy of Karen Commings.)

- **Food and water bowls**

    Shop at yard or garage sales to find unmatched dishes that people are selling literally for pennies.

- **Litter box**

    Shop at a discount department store for a dishpan that is of adequate size to use as a litter box. Another possibility is purchasing an under-the-bed storage box, with or without the lid. If the one you choose has a lid, place it under the box for some extra protection for your floor. These inexpensive products make excellent litter boxes, have higher sides to keep litter from being scattered out of them and are often cheaper than cat boxes you might find in pet stores.

- **Beds**

    Fill an old pillowcase or T-shirt with a soft piece of foam rubber. Sew the end shut. You will have a comfortable, washable cat bed.

- **Scratch posts**

    Cover a piece of wood (as small as a two-by-four-inch piece or as large as a two- to three-foot piece) with sisal rope. Place the covered wood on the floor, attach it to a door frame or put a rope handle on it and hang it from a doorknob. Or cut

SNAPSHOT:
Tahnee

Tahnee came to the Helen Opperman Krause Animal Foundation, Inc., more than ten years ago when she was only a few months old. She had a bad left eye and a sinus condition. Over and over again, she was passed up by prospective adopters because no one wanted her in her less-than-perfect condition.

When Tahnee was nine months old, shelter volunteer Eileen Wolfe decided to add her to her household, which included her husband, Mark, and four other cats. Despite her physical problems, Tahnee was active, loving and funny, according to Wolfe.

"I should have named her Kramer," says Wolfe, referring to the outlandish character on the television sitcom *Seinfeld*. Like Kramer, Tahnee slides into a room and always looks disheveled, even after a grooming session. Her sense of humor and personable manner enabled her to work her way into the number-one feline spot in the eyes of Wolfe's husband.

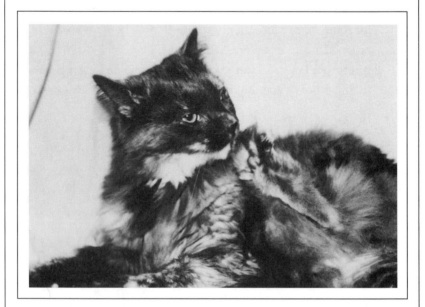

Tahnee, adopted ten years ago by Eileen Wolfe, spends some time engaging in self-grooming. (Photo courtesy of Eileen Wolfe.)

Save money with inexpensive water and food bowls from yard sales. (Photo courtesy of Karen Commings.)

corrugated cardboard strips the size of the long-side dimensions of a shoebox. Fill the box tightly with the cardboard. Sprinkle a little catnip on it, and place it on the floor for your cat to scratch.

- **Toys**

  Instead of buying toys, make them from paper grocery sacks, cardboard boxes with holes cut in them or crumpled paper tied to the end of a string (be sure to supervise the use of this last toy so that your cat does not chew on and ingest the string, which can lodge in her intestines and cause blockage). Plastic, practice golf balls are also sturdy, inexpensive toys your cat can bat around without fear of damaging herself or your belongings. Fill the foot of a mismatched sock with catnip and a little cotton stuffing, and tie off the end for an inexpensive catnip toy.

- **Grooming tools**

  Human hairbrushes and combs can be used on your cat as long as there are no sharp edges that may hurt or pull her hair. You may find these cheaper to buy initially, although buying some good-quality tools will save you money in the long run.

A CAT-FRIENDLY ENVIRONMENT

Once you bring your cat home, you will find that not only will she want to get to know you, but she also will want to explore every square inch of your house. Nothing will be outside the realm of her curiosity and need to investigate—closets, cupboards, bathroom vanities, basement storage areas, garages, bookshelves and anything else she can reach. The saying *curiosity killed the cat* has a basis in truth, so as your cat's care-giver, you will need to keep unsafe items out of her grasp, eliminate any potential dangers your house may contain and take steps to ensure that your house provides a safe, cat-friendly environment.

Household Hotspots

Cats love warm, cozy places in which to sleep or hide, and you'll find your new cat in the most out-of-the-way places. A favorite cat trick is to slip into an empty clothes dryer if the door is left open. Many a cat owner has thrown a load of clothes in the dryer and turned it on, unaware that the cat was in there sleeping. If left in the dryer, a cat will suffocate and die. To keep your cat from becoming trapped, it's best to make sure that you close the dryer door immediately after you remove a load of clothing. Never allowing your cat to sleep or play in the empty dryer in the first place is the best way to eliminate the risk of acciden-tally suffocating her. A magnet or colorful note on the front of the dryer may help remind you and others always to close the door.

Other appliances in your home present potential hazards to your cat as well. A hot oven door will burn the pads of your cat's feet if she jumps onto the door unaware of the danger. Cats detect heat by smelling the hot surface. A lowered oven door may look to your cat like a great new place to jump, and she may be unable to smell the hot surface until it's too late. It's best to close the door immediately after removing your Peking duck or veggie lasagna. Close doors immediately on toaster ovens and microwave ovens as well to keep your cat from crawling into them.

Cold Spots, Too

You never know what gastronomic delights a cat might find tempting, so it won't take long for your cat to associate the refrigerator with food, even if the food is not hers. A refrigerator door left ajar poses another hazard to the curious feline who jumps into the fridge as soon as your back is turned. To protect your cat, make sure that you close the refrigerator door as soon as you are finished taking food or drinks out of it. If you have a second refrigerator somewhere, such as in the garage or basement, make sure that its door is always closed and, if the appliance is unused, that it is sealed shut so that your cat is never able to get into it.

Cats, being the unique and often eccentric individuals that they are, may seek out new and unusual places to perform daily functions, such as drinking. A supply of fresh water is important for your cat, but she may want to imbibe somewhere besides the kitchen. The bathroom seems to be a popular way station for many felines, and having a gulp or two from the faucet of the bathroom sink satisfies their need for water and occasionally their need for play. The toilet is another favorite feline watering hole, and your cat may think it's really nifty to watch the toilet flush and then hop up and onto it and bend down to quench her thirst. Allowing your cat to drink from the sink is okay, but allowing her to drink from the toilet poses potential dangers. If your cat is small, she could fall into the toilet and drown. Because of the toilet's shape and smooth surface, there is nothing for her to grab onto and lift herself out. If you use any toilet-bowl cleaner—residue of which is left in the bowl—or a cleaner that is renewed every time you flush, you risk the danger of poisoning your cat. To be safe rather than sorry, always put the lid down on the toilet after using it. If your cat seems to like to drink in the bathroom, place a dish of water there for her to partake of at her convenience.

Other Dangers

Not all cats are chewers, and you may never have to face this potential danger, but it is important to monitor your cat to see if the attraction or habit is there to chew on dangerous electrical wires. If so, tie up loose electrical wires and place them out of sight. If you can't hide all of them, visit a hardware store and buy some plastic electrical runners into which the wires can be inserted. Plastic runners come in many colors and shapes and can be cut to size with a utility knife. Some are designed to run along baseboards, and others can run up walls or across flooring or carpet.

Make sure that all chemicals are out of your cat's reach. If you have cleaning products stashed under the kitchen or bathroom sink, make sure that your cat never goes in there to investigate. When you are using the cleaning products, wipe up any residue from surfaces that your cat walks on. Once a dangerous chemical is on your cat's hair or feet, she will lick it off and possibly poison herself. When your cat has her first veterinary visit, ask for the phone number of the nearest poison-control center in case of emergencies that might occur when the veterinarian's office is closed. As with all important phone numbers, keep it handy. Whenever possible, consider using nonchemical, natural cleaning products that are not harmful if ingested.

Other types of chemicals also pose problems. Cats are attracted to the smell of antifreeze and will drink it. Consumption of a small amount of antifreeze can produce convulsions and death. If antifreeze has spilled onto your garage floor, it poses a real hazard to your cat. Manufacturers have introduced pet-safe antifreeze on the market, but beware. Even though more of it can be ingested before reaching a deadly degree of toxicity, no antifreeze is completely safe. Clean up any antifreeze that has spilled and keep it out of the reach of your cat.

If you have a recliner in your home, make sure that your cat has not crawled up inside of it while the leg rest is extended, because she could become trapped or injured when you close it again. Dangling mini-blind cords will entice your cat to play with them. Unsuspecting cat owners have been devastated when their cats have become entangled in mini-blind cords and have been strangled to death. If you have mini-blinds in your home, cut the cord where it loops at the bottom to prevent strangulation. Tie up the excess cords to prevent your cat from chewing and ingesting them.

Looking out the window is one way your cat will amuse herself during the day, especially when you are not there or are preoccupied. Jumping at wildlife just outside the window could present a danger if your window screens are loose. Make sure that all window screens are secure, especially if you live above the first floor. Cats have a reputation for landing on their feet, but it doesn't always happen. Don't put it to the test with your cat.

Poisonous Plants

Cats love to nibble on greens. If cats are outside, they frequently chew grass. Your indoor cat will not have the option to hit on your lawn, so she may decide that your philodendron is a prime candidate to satisfy her dietary needs. No one knows for certain exactly why cats enjoy a bite or two of grass or leafy plants, but almost all of them do at one time or another.

Many common household plants are poisonous to cats if ingested. They can cause symptoms of labored breathing, nausea, vomiting, abdominal pain, diarrhea and even death. If you have any poisonous plants in your house, you should remove them or get them out of your cat's reach. That includes the dry versions of plants you may have around the house or the bouquets of flowering versions you bring inside. Some of the offenders are actually food that you might prepare for yourself or your family, such as potatoes. Keep all food that is not intended for your cat away from her.

The following are some of the more common poisonous foods and plants. Ask your veterinarian for a complete list.

Apple seeds

Apricot pits

Avocados

Bird of paradise

Black-eyed Susans

Bleeding heart

Boxwood

Bulb plants, such as amaryllis, tulips, daffodils

Burning bush

Buttercups

Caladium

Cherry pits

Chrysanthemums

Clematis

Crocuses

Crown-of-thorns

Cyclamen

Dieffenbachia

Eggplant

Elderberry

English ivy

Four-o'clocks

Foxglove

Hemlock (certain coniferous evergreen trees)

Holly

Honeysuckle

Hyacinth

Hydrangeas

Jack-in-the-pulpits

Jerusalem cherry

Jimsonweed

Larkspur

Laurel

Lily of the valley

Marigolds

Marijuana

Mistletoe

Mock orange

Monkshood

Morning glory

Mountain laurel

Mushrooms

Narcissuses

Nightshade
(including
Bittersweet)

Oleander

Peach pits

Periwinkle

Philodendrons

Poison hemlock

Poison ivy

Potatoes (raw)

Rhododendron
(including Azalea)

Skunk cabbage

Tobacco

Wisteria

Yews

KEEPING IT SIMPLE

Cats are creatures of habit, and no matter how wonderful you and your home are, your new cat will feel a little nervous and stressed in a new environment. You can make the experience of learning about you, your family and your home a positive one by helping your cat do it gradually.

You might want to consider letting your cat, especially if she is a young kitten, become familiar with your house a little at a time. This is even more important if the house is a large one and if there are lots of people or other pets in it. For the first several days, confine your cat in one area of your house, such as an extra bedroom, in which you've placed all her necessities—food and water bowls, a litter box, a bed, toys and a scratch post. Place the litter box away from the other items. Spend lots of quality time in the room with your cat, playing with her, brushing and petting her and talking to her.

In her room, provide a place for your cat to hide or just get away from it all if she needs to. She may feel frightened or be a little shy, and having a hiding place will help her feel secure. If she wants to hide, let her. Don't pull your cat out and show her to everyone. This will only add to her fear. Your goal should be to make her comfortable and not to add stress or frighten her. Give her time to adjust to her new home. Once your cat has met the members of your family and has had time to spend with you, allow her to explore the rest of your home a little at a time and at her own pace.

PROPER INTRODUCTIONS

If you have other people in your home, proper introductions are in order. Bring other family members into your cat's room, one at a time, and help them get acquainted with each other.

If small children are in the home, instruct them on how to handle the cat properly. You will want to make the experiences your children have with your cat, and all animals, positive ones. Don't let your children play roughly with or pound on the cat. They may be especially tempted to pull on your cat's tail. If your cat becomes frightened or feels threatened, she may claw or bite. As a result, your child may be injured as well as the cat, and the relationship will start out on the wrong foot for both of them. Your cat, especially if she is a kitten or young adult, is a fragile creature, and her care is in your hands.

During the first introductions, have your child seated. If the cat is small, place her in the child's lap. Allow the child to offer treats to the cat. Show the child how to gently stroke the cat in the direction in which the cat's hair is growing. Allow the cat to smell and investigate the child, and give them both time to get to know each other.

OTHER PETS IN THE HOUSE

If you're bringing a new cat into a household with other pets, it is important that you allow them to get to know each other gradually, too. If you've done your homework, you already will know that your new cat has been around the kind of pet or pets you have at home and that the relationship she had with them was positive. Obviously, it does no good to adopt a cat that had lived in a household with a dog, for example, if the dog terrorized her. Cats will generalize from one specific negative incident. Being terrorized by one dog most likely will mean that the cat will be terrified by all dogs. Do not take a new cat or kitten and hold her up to meet a dog under any circumstances. You may be imprinting a fear on your cat that will last her entire life.

Allow your cat and dog to learn about each other by scent. A useful technique is to place your dog's food bowl near the door to the cat's room. By allowing them to eat near each other, they will become familiar with each other's scents by performing a positive activity—

Cats and dogs, such as these at the San Francisco SPCA, can coexist peacefully with a little planning and patience. (Photo courtesy of the San Francisco SPCA.)

eating. Once they have investigated each other through closed doors, allow them to interact in a controlled setting. Leash your dog and command it to sit or stay while in your cat's room. You will be able to tell from your cat's behavior how interested she is in getting to know your dog. If the cat wants to hide, let her. If she wants to come forward and investigate Rover, allow her to do that also—all the while holding your dog to keep it from lunging at or frightening the cat. You also will want to make sure your cat doesn't lunge at your dog and possibly scratch it or bite it. Offering them both treats may help to ease the situation. During the introduction period, it is best not to allow the two animals to become familiar with each other without your presence. And, until you are absolutely positive that both animals will be safe in each other's company, keep them separated when no one is home.

Much has been written about the correct way to introduce a new cat to a cat already living in the household. Regardless of the method, a gradual learning process is the most effective. Your resident cat will feel like the whole house is her territory, so you want to assure her that the newcomer will not be an infringement on her space. Accordingly, lots of extra tender loving care is in order during this process.

Use the same technique described in the preceding section by allowing the cats to become familiar with each other's scents through the door to the newcomer's room. Again, place food bowls for each of them on either side of the door at mealtimes. When it is time to allow the newcomer to explore the house, put the resident cat in the newcomer's room to investigate the scents in there. Some cats will like each other immediately, while others may take days, weeks or even months to develop a relationship. Be patient with them and let them become friends in their own time. You must make sure, however, that no fights erupt and that no one comes to harm. Again, as with proper introductions with a canine, keep the cats separated when you are not at home until you are sure they can coexist peacefully.

Animals of different species can adapt to each other, but it is best done when they are young. If the animals are of different sizes or temperaments, caution must be taken to make sure that they are compatible and that neither animal is injured by the other. Your parakeet may look like dinner to your cat, who is a hunter at heart, so if you have a bird, better keep it out of Kitty's reach or know beforehand that your cat can exist peacefully with birds and that your bird will not die of fright just from seeing a cat in the house. If you have small mammals, such as gerbils, mice or hamsters, provide them with plenty of protective coverings to keep them away from the cat, and keep the fish tanks covered to protect the fish and to prevent your cat from falling in.

THE NAME'S THE THING

Your cat may have had a name while she was at the shelter. If the name suits you and your cat, keep it. If you would like to give your cat another name, choose what you will call her in the first few days and speak her name to her often. You will find that your cat learns her name rather quickly. As time goes on, you most likely will have other nicknames that come to mind, some of which may be based on the cute things she does.

SNAPSHOT:
Rubin

Rubin had three strikes against him when he entered the Helen Opperman Krause Animal Foundation: He was old (between twelve and thirteen years). He suffered from *hyperthyroidism*—a condition caused by overactivity of the thyroid gland, resulting in a plethora of symptoms that include severe weight loss, hyperactivity and possible heart problems. And, his longhaired coat was so matted that it had to be shaved, revealing his thin frame. Most cats with problems such as Rubin's don't stand a chance of finding a home, much less a good one.

But pet lovers Steve and Tim Barker immediately recognized Rubin's potential to become a loving member of their family and decided to adopt him into their home (which also included three other resident cats, a Saint Bernard, three parakeets, a cockatoo and a canary).

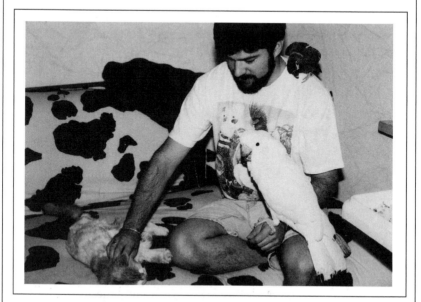

Rubin relaxes with Steve Barker, a cockatoo named Suzie and a parakeet named Cody. (Photo courtesy of Karen Commings.)

"We thought no one else would want him in his condition," says Steve Barker about the friendly cat who followed them around the shelter crying at the top of his lungs. But by observing Rubin in teract with the other shelter cats, Steve and Tim predicted that the lovable Rubin would have no trouble assimilating with their creature companions.

Once home, the Barkers discovered that Rubin had yet another problem—he appeared to be very hard of hearing. Instead of simply meowing, Rubin bellows, just as he did at the shelter. When Steve and Tim communicate with him, they must do the same.

Rubin is medicated twice daily to fight his hyperthyroid condition, but he has adapted well to life in his new home. The other cats, the dog and the myriad birds are neither threatening nor threatened. In spite of his physical problems, Rubin's ability to offer his human owners the same love and affection as a cat in perfect physical condition shines through.

Your cat will learn those nicknames, too. A cat is capable of responding to three, four or more names, as long as she is frequently addressed by those names.

When choosing a name, select one that is complimentary and highlights your cat's good qualities. Avoid a name that is derogatory—one that causes your friends to burst into fits of laughter when they meet her or one that is embarrassing every time a receptionist calls you and your cat into your veterinary appointment. Cats are sensitive to being laughed at and embarrass easily, so be sure to give your cat a name that she can be proud of. Many cat owners select "people" names for their cats, and such a name may be preferable to you if you would rather have a Greta or a Chuckie bounding around the house than a Sparky or a Pepper.

Cat naming is part art, part science. Cats respond more easily to names that contain a few hard consonants. Names like Dusty, Rocky, Patty or Carla are easier for a cat to learn than names such as Feather, Helen, Sean or Michele. Sometimes, an appropriate name will just pop into your head, and in a single moment, you will have found the perfect name for your cat.

SELECTING A VETERINARIAN

Shortly after bringing your shelter cat home, make an appointment with a veterinarian to have her examined. Don't wait until you have an emergency to establish a relationship with a veterinarian. A veterinarian will give priority treatment to existing clients, and some may have periods of time when they are not able to take on new clients. Finding a veterinarian with whom you want to establish a long-term relationship will help ensure that your cat always gets the care she needs when she needs it.

Veterinarians are required to have a college degree and at least three years of study in an accredited veterinary school. Veterinarians also must be licensed in the state in which they practice. To keep abreast of current veterinary medical trends, veterinarians will join professional groups such as the American Veterinary Medical Association or the American Association of Feline Practitioners.

There are many types of veterinary practices from which to choose. Some treat all animals, while others specialize in only small animals—cats, dogs and rabbits, for example. Other veterinarians have set up practices dedicated solely to treating felines. Some veterinarians specialize in holistic medicine, adding treatments such as acupuncture, homeopathy, herbal medicine and chiropractic to traditional forms of treatment. Still others make house calls. If transportation or lack of it is a factor for you, finding a veterinarian who will come to you will be important.

As a consumer, you will need to shop around to find the type of veterinary practice that suits your needs. You will find many veterinarians listed in the Yellow Pages. You may also want to ask shelter personnel for recommendations or ask friends or co-workers who have pets who their veterinarian is and why they like him or her. If you must drive to a veterinarian's office, finding one that is nearby may be important to you. Whatever your criteria, don't feel obligated to stay with the first veterinarian you talk to. The veterinarian will want to make sure the relationship is a lasting one as much as you will. As important as it is to find the right cat, it is just as important to find the right veterinarian who will help you care for your cat for her entire life.

When you are selecting a veterinarian, call and ask to interview him or her. Prepare a list of questions before your visit, and write down the responses so that you can do comparative shopping. Inquire about the office hours—if you work out of the home, being able to make appointments during the evenings or on weekends might be important.

Ask how the veterinarian handles emergencies and off-hours problems that require immediate treatment. Some veterinarians are available for their clients whenever they have emergency situations. Other veterinarians will refer you to 24-hour emergency clinics when their practices are closed. If this is the case, obtain the location of the emergency service. If you've chosen a veterinarian because of his or her geographic proximity, an emergency clinic in the next county won't serve your needs. Make sure that you are comfortable with both the veterinarian and his or her emergency services.

Visit the veterinarian's office. What does the waiting room look like? Is it clean, or are there remnants of Fido's or Fluffy's visits on the floor and furniture? Is the office personnel helpful and courteous? If the practice treats all types of animals, is there a separate waiting area for cats? Cats become stressed at the vet, and having loud, barking dogs sitting next to the cat carrier or sniffing the carrier's contents can add a level of anxiety that will only make treating your cat more difficult. This stress can be avoided when the veterinarian sits dogs on one side of the waiting area and cats on the other and insists that dogs be on a leash and under control by their owners. Such a simple thing may make the difference between whether your cat tolerates a vet visit or spends her time there in fear and cowering in the back of her carrier.

Ask to see the hospital area. Are dogs and cats housed separately? The same types of mixed occupants can cause added anxiety for your cat if she must spend some time in the hospital after surgery or recovering from illness.

When you take your cat to the veterinarian for an appointment, prepare for the visit. Veterinarians should give you enough of their time so that your questions can be answered, but you must be respectful of their time as well. They will not appreciate trying to determine what is wrong with your cat if you can't tell them what the symptoms are or why you believe that your cat is sick. If your cat has not eaten, write down the date and time of her last meal. If she has been vomiting, note when and describe it. Because your cat won't be able to tell the vet where it hurts, she must rely on you to do it for her. Nothing is more frustrating for a veterinarian than trying to squeeze information about an animal's condition out of her owner.

When you take your cat for her first veterinary visit, talk to the veterinarian about tests for any contagious diseases that were not done at the shelter from which you adopted her. To help you communicate with your veterinarian and help him provide the best possible care, make a checklist of your cat's medical status based on your knowledge of her from the shelter. What shots has she had, for example, and what dates were they administered? Was she spayed? Was she tested for *feline leukemia virus* (FeLV) or *feline immunodeficiency virus* (FIV)? If the shelter gave you a copy of her records while she was there, take them with you. Most veterinarians require new clients to fill out a form when they bring in a pet, so having the necessary information about your cat will help you provide the information.

Finding a veterinarian with whom you can communicate will aid in the proper care of your cat and help ensure that she lives a long time.

CHAPTER 6

Cat Care Basics

One of the best ways to ensure that you and your cat spend many quality years together is to provide him with the best in health care. Regular veterinary visits, good nutrition and good grooming will play an important part in the care you give him.

START WITH GOOD GROOMING

Cats have a reputation for cleanliness, and this is not unfounded. Cats spend a good many of their waking hours grooming themselves—after meals, before bedtime or catnaps or whenever the mood strikes them. You may notice your cat, on those rare occasions when he acts klutzy instead of with the gracefulness for which cats are noted, seizing the moment to lick his hair a few times, seemingly embarrassed by his clumsiness.

Grooming keeps a cat's coat clean and shiny. A well-kept coat is a sign of a healthy cat, and one of the signals that a cat does not feel well is that he will stop grooming himself.

Hairball Prevention

Cats wash themselves by licking their hair with their tongues, which are covered with tiny projections called *papillae*.

103

These give a cat's tongue its rough feel. You'll notice its gravelly texture when your cat decides to wash you once in a while instead of himself. Mutual grooming is a sign of affection among cats, so don't feel offended if your cat gives you a few licks as he's also washing himself. It's a compliment.

To wash hard-to-reach places, such as faces and whiskers, cats will lick their feet and run the dampened foot over the surfaces to be washed. They will spread their toes and spend time cleaning between them and the pads on their feet.

Since cats are so good at keeping themselves clean, you may wonder why it is necessary to assist them in their grooming efforts. I've already emphasized the need to brush your cat at least once a week to help him remove excess hair. All cats shed to some degree. As new hair grows, old hair dies and becomes loose. If you do not brush your cat regularly, he will ingest the shedding hair as he washes. When a cat ingests too much hair, hairballs form in his stomach or elsewhere along the digestive tract. If the hairball passes, it will be expelled in the cat's feces through normal digestive processes. Cats also vomit hairballs.

But if the ingested hair builds up, it can create problems in the digestive tract and, in severe circumstances, require surgery to remove. Regular brushing and combing will help prevent this problem.

In addition to regular brushing, you should give your cat a hairball remedy even if you groom your cat weekly. You can find hairball remedies in pet stores or get them from your veterinarian. If you prefer, or especially if your cat prefers, offer him some butter or petroleum jelly several times a week or put a little vegetable oil (about one quarter of a teaspoon) in his wet food.

Brushing Teeth

A regular once- or twice-weekly grooming session will give you the opportunity to inspect your cat's mouth and brush his teeth. Improper dental care can result in periodontal disease that may ultimately result in your cat losing his teeth. You won't be able to fit your cat with kitty dentures, so prevention is the best way to ensure that your cat keeps on chewing.

The buildup of tartar on your cat's teeth can cause all sorts of problems as your cat ages. The presence of bacteria in his mouth can spread to other organs, such as the kidneys and heart, causing damage to more than Kitty's smile. Your veterinarian will scrape away minor tartar on the teeth as part of an annual exam, but a more serious buildup will require your cat to be anesthetized for a cleaning.

You can help prevent tooth and gum disease by adhering to a regular brushing schedule. Keep your cat's teeth clean by using a specially designed cat toothbrush and toothpaste developed for felines. Never use toothpaste made for people to brush your cat's teeth.

Bonding

In addition to preventing hairballs, regular grooming will help you bond with your cat and accustom him to being handled. Grooming should be a positive experience—one that is anticipated joyfully by both of you. Set aside a time that is consistent and unhurried to groom your cat.

During each grooming session, talk to your cat. Offer treats so that he will associate grooming with another pleasant activity—eating. Grooming, and the talking and petting that accompanies it, helps boost your cat's self-esteem.

Clipping Claws

Your shelter cat will most likely come with his claws intact. As with their hair, cats shed their claws, too. As the sheath of the old claw dies, the new claw grows, pushing the deadened portion out. Cats scratch to remove the deadened claws, and you undoubtedly will observe your cat pulling off the sheaths of his claws with his teeth when he grooms himself. Clipping your cat's claws not only will make him more comfortable but also will help prevent damage to your furniture if you have not provided him with a scratching alternative.

Examine your cat's claws during regular grooming sessions. If they appear too long, use a clipper specifically designed for cats to remove the tips. Gently spread your cat's toes to distend the claws. Insert the claw into the clipper and press the handle. Be careful to cut only the tip of the claw, not the quick. If you cut the quick, the claw will bleed and be painful to your cat. The *quick* is a pinkish area near the top of the claw. If you are uncertain how to clip your cat's claws, ask your veterinarian to show you.

Some cat owners declaw their cats to prevent them from scratching furniture or people. Declawing involves surgically removing the end bone of the toe that contains the claw. Some veterinarians remove only the last digit, but others remove more. Most often, cat owners have only the claws on the front feet of their cats removed, but occasionally a pet owner will ask to have the claws removed from the back feet as well.

After the surgery, the wound is either sutured or sealed with surgical glue, and the cat's paws are taped or bound until the incision heals. Declawing is performed while the animal is under anesthesia and can be done at the same time that a cat is spayed or neutered.

Following the declawing surgery, a cat should use only special litter-box filler for seven to ten days. This special litter is designed so that it will not get into the cat's toes and the wounds when he uses the box. Discuss with your veterinarian what kinds of litter pose no threat to your cat's healing process following declawing.

Declawing is an issue that is hotly debated among cat owners. People in favor of it say that it is better to declaw a cat than to give him up or let him run outside to alleviate his clawing behavior. They point to the fact that veterinarians perform this surgery, so it must be safe. People opposed to declawing say that the surgery is painful and causes irreparable emotional harm to the declawed cat.

An alternative to declawing that is recommended by some veterinarians and animal behaviorists is a product called Soft Paws™. Soft Paws are caps that can be inserted onto your cat's claws to prevent unwanted scratching. Two or three Soft Paws will fall off within a month, but you can simply replace them with new ones. Soft Paws are safe, effective and have no harmful side effects on your cat.

Before you decide, discuss the pros and cons of declawing with your veterinarian. Ultimately, if it means the difference between your cat keeping his good home and being given up to someone else, declawing may be the only alternative. If you decide to declaw your cat, be aware of the potential problems it may create, and be careful to follow your veterinarian's advice following surgery. Be extra careful not to allow a declawed cat outside, because he won't be able to defend himself or to escape a predator by climbing a tree.

Bathing

Because cats are so good at keeping themselves clean, many cat owners and cat experts feel that bathing a cat on a regular basis is unnecessary. Many cats do not like water, and a bath can be a traumatic experience. If you have adopted a kitten, it is preferable that you bathe him occasionally when he is young so that he becomes accustomed to the water. If you must bathe him to alleviate a skin condition or to get rid of fleas later on, the bath will not be an ordeal.

To bathe a cat, fill the sink with a few inches of water. Place a towel or rubber mat on the bottom for your cat to hold onto. If you prefer, place a screen over the sink and place your cat on it. Bath and rinse water will fall below into the sink, and your cat will not feel submerged in the water. By using a screen, your cat will have something to sink his claws into besides you.

Use only shampoo that is intended for cats. Do not use Fido's doggy shampoo, your own shampoo or a substance such as dish detergent to bathe your cat. Any of these products may contain chemicals that are toxic to cats. Once your cat is wet, massage a little shampoo into his hair, being careful not to get any into his eyes, mouth or nose. Rinse the shampoo thoroughly out of his hair and towel dry. If your cat is calm and has a more laid-back personality, you might want to try drying his hair with a hair dryer set on low. Some cats have an aversion to loud noises, so if you think your cat may flip from the hair dryer, don't use it. Bath time is also to be a positive experience, and you don't want to make it a stressful time by adding a component that makes your cat anxious.

If your cat will not tolerate water, use a dry shampoo available at pet stores. If you want to remove some odor from your cat's hair, rub some baking soda into his hair and brush it out. It will leave his hair clean-smelling and will not pose a problem if he ingests some of the baking soda when he washes himself. Be sure to monitor your pet when using dry shampoos to make sure that he is not allergic to them.

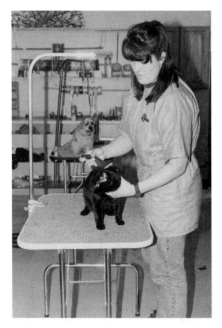

Sometimes a cat needs the services of a professional groomer. (Photo courtesy of Karen Commings.)

Tools of the Trade

Chapter 5, "Bringing Home Baby," mentioned the importance of purchasing a good-quality pet brush and comb and using them regularly. In addition, you will need a claw clipper to clip your cat's claws and cat shampoo if you intend to bathe your cat. Other grooming tools you may need are a slicker brush, an undercoat rake and a flea comb.

A *slicker brush* is a flat, metal brush with wire bristles of about one half inch along its surface. Slicker brushes should be used on shorthaired cats to remove dead skin particles and stimulate the flow of a cat's natural oils. Grooming first with a slicker brush and then following it with a soft-bristled brush will help make your cat's coat shiny and smooth.

An *undercoat rake* looks very much like a mini-rake that you might use for gathering up leaves in your yard. Longhaired cats and those with thick coats will benefit from the use of an undercoat rake, which typically thins and removes the thick underhair and helps keep it from knotting. Trying to brush out knots in a cat's coat can pull the cat's skin and make your cat irritable. Knots are difficult to remove and doing so is painful for the cat, so it is best to prevent them from forming.

A *flea comb* is a metal comb that has fine teeth that are close together. The purpose of the flea comb is to help remove fleas by trapping them in the teeth of the comb. Once the flea is on the comb, it should be dipped in a cup of flea shampoo or removed and smashed with a tissue.

PROFILE:
LOOKING GOOD

Getting a bath or having his hair completely shaved off may not be on the top of your cat's list of priorities, but feeling more comfortable and enabling him to combat disease just might be. Cats arriving at the Denver Dumb Friends League (DDFL) with coats that are severely matted, dirty or flea-infested are given a new lease on life by visiting the league's Grooming Center, where their hair and their personalities get the chance to shine.

Dealing with a matted coat can be painful and stressful, so animals coming into the Grooming Center receive a little extra love and affection from the groomers. Once they have been cleaned up, the animals are typically perkier and more responsive. Not intended to simply make the animals look cute, the DDFL Grooming Center gives cats and dogs that have been neglected a chance to look and feel better and also increases their likelihood of being adopted.

The DDFL Grooming Center grooms more than 2,000 animals annually, of which about 25 percent are cats. Longhaired cats typically suffer the most when their hair is neglected. The DDFL has one full-time groomer who is given lots of help from volunteers.

Professional Services

You may find occasions when, despite your good grooming efforts, your cat needs the services of a professional groomer. If a cat is not accustomed to being groomed from a young age, he may resist the process when he is older, making it more difficult to prevent the buildup of knots in his hair or to prevent ingestion of too much hair.

Before taking your cat to any professional groomer, make sure that the groomer has been trained to groom cats. Typically, groomers who advertise in the Yellow Pages specify whether they are qualified to groom cats.

A cat groomer will know how to handle your cat, be sensitive to his needs and be familiar with products intended to be used on cats. Do not allow your cat to be groomed by someone who uses products designed only for use on dogs.

HOME HEALTH EXAM

One of the major benefits of grooming—aside from helping your cat maintain a clean, healthy appearance—is that the grooming session gives you an opportunity to perform a home health exam. By checking your cat regularly for problems that may develop, you will catch them early when they can be treated more successfully.

Ears, Eyes and Mouth

Healthy ears will be pink and clean. If you see black specks or a dark brown, soil-like substance in your cat's ears, it is a sign that he may have ear mites. Other signs of ear-mite infestations are shaking the head or pawing at the ears. If you keep your cat indoors, it is unlikely that he will contract ear mites, but he may have caught them in his previous living conditions.

Mites are microscopic parasites that build up in a cat's ears. They are relatively easy to eradicate and should be treated immediately upon detection. Ear mites lay eggs that can hatch later, so be certain to treat your cat long enough to get rid of the mites and the eggs. You also should be sure to treat *both* ears, even if only one ear appears to be infected. Cats can transfer the mites from one ear to the other during cleaning, shaking or scratching. Mites are contagious, so treat all other cats you have to prevent the spread of the infestation.

As with all parasitic infections, the sooner you begin treatment, the more successful the treatment will be. Waiting too long can also bring on more severe health problems for your cat. If you detect ear mites, have your cat examined by a veterinarian.

Cats have excellent eyesight, even in the low-light conditions that leave humans stumbling in the dark. You may notice on occasion your cat's eyes glowing like oncoming headlights. The glow, which has an eerie quality, is actually the reflection of an ambient light source bounced off the layer of reflective cells at the back of your cat's eyes.

Cats have an eyelid and an inner eyelid that protects each eye. A scratch or contracted illness, such as conjunctivitis, can cause the inner eyelid to be exposed and to become red. Such a condition should be seen and treated by a veterinarian immediately. Neurological problems may result in the dilation of a cat's eyes in a well-lighted environment or unequal dilation of a cat's pupils.

If you notice a buildup of dirt in the corner of your cat's eyes, simply wipe it off with your finger

A technician applies eye ointment to a cat at the PeopleSoft Pet Recovery Center at the San Francisco SCPA. (Photo courtesy of the San Francisco SPCA.)

or a soft cloth. Such a condition is not harmful. If you detect tearing, it may be a sign that your cat has a piece of dirt or dust in his eye. This should clear in a day or so, but if it persists, have your cat examined by your veterinarian.

Examine your cat's teeth and gums. His teeth should be white, and his gums should be pink. As they age, cats will experience tartar buildup on their teeth. Good dental care is as important as proper nutrition and other types of health care. If you detect tartar on your cat's teeth or reddened gums, discuss the problem with your veterinarian. He or she may recommend that you brush your cat's teeth with a toothbrush and toothpaste developed for use with cats. For cats who do not particularly enjoy having their teeth brushed, there are dental-care products that can be squirted into your cat's mouth to help keep tartar to a minimum. As your cat ages, discuss having his teeth cleaned professionally by your veterinarian. This is done under an anesthetic, but it can be done on an outpatient basis, so there is no need to have your cat stay in the hospital overnight.

Coat and Skin

Examine your cat's coat as part of regular grooming sessions. His coat should be clean and shiny. Some external conditions, such as warm weather, may make him groom less often, but if self-grooming has stopped for more than a day or two, it may be a sign that your cat is ill.

The skin is the largest organ of the cat's body. Skin problems can be caused by a number of things, such as bacterial or viral infections, injuries, contact with chemicals or poisons, parasites, stress, allergies, tumors and frostbite. If left untreated, skin problems can become serious. As you are grooming your cat, feel his skin with your hands. Do you detect any bumps or lumps under his coat? Do you see any hair loss, redness or swelling? If you find any signs of skin problems, have your cat examined by a veterinarian.

Fleas

If you detect specks resembling salt and pepper in your cat's coat, it is a sign that he has fleas. The specks are bits of flea feces, eggs and undigested blood that the fleas deposit after biting your cat. Even keeping your cat indoors is no guarantee that he will not get fleas. Fleas can be carried in from the yard on clothing and other pets. Fleas are by far the most common parasite to inflict cats.

Fleas should be treated immediately upon detection. There is a wide variety of flea products on the market—pills, sprays, powders, shampoos, flea collars, soap and a newer product that is a disposable dampened cloth similar to those designed for travelers. Some products contain chemicals and some contain natural ingredients reputed to control fleas. Discuss with your veterinarian what product is best for your cat and your situation. Use the product according to package directions, and because combining flea products can be toxic, never use a mix of products on your cat.

To effectively treat the problem, you must eliminate the fleas and larvae from your cat and also from your home. Flea larvae, or eggs, can live up to two years in carpet and furniture, so even if your cat does not have fleas at the time of adoption, he stands a chance of contracting them if an animal in your home previously had fleas that were not totally eliminated. Products available to eliminate fleas from the home include foggers, premises sprays and carpet sprays. Using a fogger requires that you and every other living thing, including plants, leave the home while the fogger is working. Some premises sprays allow you to remain in the house but do not allow your cat to walk on a surface that has been sprayed until it is dry. This method enables you to disinfect one room at a time while you place your cat in a safe location as you spray from room to room and wait for each consecutive room to dry. Depending on the severity of the infestation, you may have to perform the eradication measures more than once to kill the fleas and larvae.

If you are so inclined, a good preventive measure would be to use a premises spray on your carpet and upholstered furniture prior to bringing your new cat home. Any fleas or flea eggs that are on your cat will jump or fall off and die. Or, if you plan to keep your new cat isolated for a few days until he becomes accustomed to your home and family, treat the room in which he will stay before you bring him home.

Some cats develop allergies to flea bites, and a flea infestation will cause the cat to engage in excessive self-grooming. He may even develop bald spots as a result. Early detection and removal of fleas from the cat and the home are extremely important as a general rule but especially in such situations. Once the cat has developed the excessive licking habit, it is more difficult to treat, and the overgrooming may continue long after the last flea has passed into the great beyond.

The presence of fleas on your cat is an indication that he may well have tapeworms. Tapeworms are caused by the cat's ingestion of flea dirt. The tapeworm lives in the digestive tract of a cat and is noticeable when segments resembling rice or sesame seeds leave the body. Tapeworms can be treated easily, but to rid them entirely means ridding your cat and your house of the flea infestation. Left untreated, tapeworms can rob your cat of good nutrition, weaken his immune system and leave him susceptible to other ailments.

OTHER PARASITES

In addition to ear mites and fleas, your cat can contract other parasites. Some are visible on the surface of the skin, while others are internal and can only be detected when they leave the body. Keeping your cat indoors will reduce the risk of contracting these parasites, but your cat may have contracted them before you adopted him, so knowing how to address such problems is important. These conditions are treatable, so if you suspect any parasitic problems with your new cat, discuss medications with your veterinarian.

Roundworms

Toxocara cati and *Toxascaris leonina,* commonly called *roundworms,* live in the small intestines of cats. Roundworms are contagious. The most common form of transmission is from a mother cat to her kittens, although cats living in communal situations can contract roundworms by ingesting the eggs. Cats can pass the worms in their stools, where they may go unnoticed by you unless you take a stool sample to your veterinarian regularly as part of your cat's annual checkup. Cats also can vomit the worms. When vomited, the worms resemble strings of spaghetti that will straighten out from their circular form as they die once out of the cat's body.

The presence of roundworms is usually not life-threatening, and your cat can be treated with medication. Be sure to get the appropriate medication from your veterinarian, because some over-the-counter dewormers are very toxic.

Hookworms

Like roundworms, hookworms live in the intestines of cats, although they are somewhat rare. Kittens can become infected by the passage of hookworm larvae through their mother's milk. Adult cats can contract hookworms by ingesting the larvae in contaminated soil or by larvae penetrating the skin. Hookworms can weaken the intestinal walls and permit blood to seep into the intestine, ultimately resulting in anemia.

Infected cats may have black stools that are tarry in consistency. You even may notice blood in the stools. Treatment with a dewormer will bring about recovery.

Ticks

Although an indoor cat will rarely experience ticks, be aware of their existence if you allow your cat to go outdoors. If you allow your cat outside on a leash, he could be bitten by a tick. A tick will look like a tiny bump on the skin. It can be removed with a pair of tweezers.

In most cases, ticks are not harmful, but be aware that the deer tick can carry Lyme disease, which can infect cats as well as humans and other animals. If you suspect that your cat has a tick on his body, or if you've removed one, show it to your veterinarian to make sure that it is not a Lyme disease–carrying tick.

Ringworm

Ringworm is not a worm but a fungal infection that appears as circular, hairless regions usually on the head and neck. Ringworm is highly contagious and can be transmitted from animals to humans. Ringworm is most commonly found in the head and limb areas. If your cat has ringworm, you may notice circular areas of hair loss or baldness, areas of fluid-filled sacks or pigment alterations.

Ringworm should be treated immediately with topical medications, and infected areas of your home should be cleaned to prevent the infection from spreading. Cats with ringworm should be isolated from other members of the household until they are well. Ringworm is usually seen on cats with immune-system problems. If your cat has ringworm, he should be tested for diseases such as feline leukemia virus or feline immunodeficiency virus.

SPAYING AND NEUTERING

Having your female cat spayed or your male cat neutered was emphasized earlier in this book as a way to accomplish several goals. An altered cat (one who is spayed or neutered) will likely live longer than an unaltered one and have less risk of contracting reproductive disorders, such as ovarian or mammary cancer. In addition to the purely physical benefits, an altered cat will not exhibit the behaviors associated with reproduction, such as spraying to mark territory or heat-related behaviors that owners find so annoying.

It is commonly believed that only male cats spray, but females can spray as well, and females that are in heat often lose control of their bladder function and will dribble out of the litter box at inopportune times. Male cats wail when fighting over a female in heat. You might have heard two males pairing off at night; the eerie noises they make sound like the frightened cries of a child. Females will yowl and walk around with their rear ends in the air, exposing them to any male that happens to be available, regardless of whether the male has been neutered. Owners of intact cats will find these behaviors extremely annoying, and altering greatly reduces the risk of a cat exhibiting such behaviors.

Spaying is an operation that is performed under anesthesia. The technical name for spaying is *ovariohysterectomy*, and it involves the removal of a cat's ovaries, oviducts and uterus. A cat that has been spayed may be required to stay at the veterinarian's facility for one or two days. About ten days later, she must return for removal of her stitches.

Neutering, or castration, is also performed under anesthesia, but it can be done on an outpatient basis. In most cases, you will be able to pick up your male cat the same day, as long as your veterinarian has determined that it is safe for your cat to go home. Because no stitches are involved in the neutering surgery, you will not have to return later, as you will if you have had your female cat spayed.

Cat owners cite many, often frivolous, reasons for not spaying or neutering their cats. Some believe their cats will become fat and lazy if altered, but it is overeating and lack of exercise that adds unwanted pounds to Kitty's frame, not altering.

Some cat owners feel that they are depriving their cats if they have them altered. For a cat, reproduction is a biological function and has no emotional ramifications. Even though a female cat will feed, care for and protect her young, she will not sit around pining about missing the joys of motherhood if she does not have a litter of kittens. Your male cat won't resent you for not letting him go out and have a great time fighting with other male cats over a female in heat. Both male and female cats will have more fun sitting on your lap or playing with a catnip toy than engaging in reproductive activities.

Another reason some pet owners give for not having their pets altered is that they want their human children to experience the miracle of birth. While birth is a miracle and a joy to behold, there is an ugly, tragic side to this event. Every year, millions of cats are put to death in shelters across the country because there are not enough homes for them. For every cat that is brought into the world indiscriminately, another cat dies somewhere, alone and unwanted.

If a child is to see the miracle of birth, should he or she not be exposed to the tragedy of death that bringing unwanted pets into the world causes? If children are to be part of an educational program that provides them with an appreciation of life and all living things, why not take them to a shelter to see the many animals housed there or allow them to become involved in the shelter's programs? This is far more compassionate than forcing your cat companion to have kittens and increasing her risk of getting other illnesses. Once involved, your children will see more than their share of birth miracles and get a sense of the whole picture.

Don't delay spaying or neutering your cat. Female cats can mate and bear kittens as young as the age of six months and occasionally do so at an even younger age. One female, if left intact, has the potential to be responsible for the births of more than 420,000 kittens in seven years, according to The Humane Society of the United States. One female can have as many as four litters per season. Each litter can contain as many as six kittens. Each of her offspring is capable of having the same number. As staggering as those figures are, you must realize that each litter bears additional litters until the geometric progression results in a phenomenal number of kittens and cats, most of which will live short, suffering lives and die homeless.

Cats typically are altered at about six months of age. In recent years, veterinarians have been performing spaying and neutering surgeries on younger cats—sometimes on cats as young as six weeks. The safety of performing these surgeries on very young cats is a hotly debated issue within the veterinary community. No-kill shelters alter animals that are of age prior to adopting them out to help fight the overpopulation problem. Anyone adopting kittens must sign an agreement that they will have the animal altered as soon as he is of age. Adopting a cat that has been altered will eliminate the need for you to incur this expense, unless the shelter asks you to contribute toward the surgery at the time of adoption.

PROFILE:
As Easy As A-B-C

Financial difficulties, lack of transportation, inability to find low-cost spay and neuter surgeries. These are some of the hurdles pet owners encounter that deter them from having their pets altered. The Animal Friends Animal Birth Control (ABC) Spay/Neuter Coordination Center attempts to remove any obstacles that prevent people from having this important surgery performed on their pets and makes it possible for every pet owner.

Founded in 1993, the ABC Coordination Center works with thirty-five participating veterinarians in five Western Pennsylvania counties to establish cost ceilings for spaying and neutering and subsidizes the surgery for owners who cannot afford the reduced fees. Pet owners are asked to contribute according to their ability to pay. The combined average controlled cost for altering a pet, including cats and dogs, through the ABC Center is $39.00, and the center has been providing an average subsidy of $18.00 to needy families.

Many beneficiaries of ABC Coordination Center services include senior citizens and families on public assistance. The ABC Coordination Center offers transportation to any of the participating veterinarians for pet owners who cannot get to one of them on their own.

Inspired by the San Francisco SPCA's goal of finding homes for every adoptable animal, the ABC Coordination Center began as a means of addressing the staggering number of pets euthanized in the region every year. An estimated 25,000 unwanted animals were put to death in Allegheny County alone to the tune of $750,000.00 in taxpayer money. The ABC Coordination Center is open for referrals six days a week, and in the first two years of its existence, the center has scheduled over 5,000 cats and dogs for spay/neuter surgery, saving an estimated 15,000 animals from eventual euthanasia.

Shelters that euthanize often do not alter animals to avoid incurring additional expense for cats and dogs that will be put to death. They do, however, require that the new pet owner spay or neuter any unaltered pet and in some cases require that the pet parent pay the spay/neuter fee at the time of adoption. The shelter then gives the pet parent a voucher to be redeemed at participating veterinary practices. Regardless of the type of shelter from which you adopt and the method for handling unaltered cats, if your special cat is not altered when you adopt him, you will be required to do so. More and more shelters are contracting with veterinarians to perform this important surgery prior to adopting out any of the cats in their care.

Spaying and neutering are so important that low-cost spaying and neutering organizations have burst onto the animal scene all over the country. If you would like to find one in your area, talk to the shelter from which you are adopting your cat. If the shelter staff is unaware of any such group, see Chapter 10, "Resources."

AN OUNCE OF PREVENTION

The old adage *an ounce of prevention is worth a pound of cure* certainly applies to caring for your cat as well as to caring for yourself. Maintaining your cat's good health and detecting problems while they are easily treatable is not only more humane to your cat but also more efficient and cost-effective for you.

One of the primary ways you can increase your cat's health and well-being and reduce veterinary medical costs is by providing your cat with an annual physical checkup. As part of a regular exam, your veterinarian will take your cat's temperature; listen to his heartbeat; examine his ears, eyes and mouth; look for any problems with his teeth; feel for any lumps or bumps on his body and perform a fecal exam (if you have brought along a stool sample). Your veterinarian will let you know of any abnormalities and how you should handle them.

As part of an annual checkup, your veterinarian will administer vaccinations for some common contagious diseases. Feline distemper is a viral disease that most often affects kittens, although it can affect cats of any age. Feline distemper is transmitted by direct contact with infected cats or contaminated objects, such as food bowls and litter pans.

The staff at the PeopleSoft Pet Recovery Center at the San Francisco SPCA provides a medical exam for an incoming cat that includes listening to his heart rate. (Photo courtesy of the San Francisco SPCA.)

Several respiratory diseases, such as feline calicivirus and feline herpes virus, cause acute infections in cats. Respiratory infections are extremely contagious, because they are airborne viruses and can pass quickly from one cat to another. Although respiratory viruses pose no danger to humans, you can infect your cat by transmitting the virus from your clothes if you have come into contact with cats that are infected. If you have been in contact with infected cats, it is best to wash yourself and your clothing before handling your cat.

Although not all respiratory diseases are preventable through vaccinations, you will be able to keep your cat from contracting feline distemper and the respiratory viruses mentioned here by keeping him on a regular vaccination schedule.

Depending on what state you live in, you may be required by law to obtain a rabies shot for your cat. Rabies attacks an animal's central nervous system and is transmitted through the saliva in a bite from an infected animal. Cats left out to run are at risk of being bitten by rabid animals, especially in certain parts of the country. Even if your shelter cat will be staying indoors, protection is important in the event that he ever gets out. Your veterinarian will give your cat an annual rabies shot as part of his annual checkup.

WARNING SIGNS OF ILLNESS

As your cat's caregiver, you will want to monitor him on an ongoing basis and pay close attention to any signs or symptoms that something is wrong. Look at the symptoms in context of the whole animal. For example, did your cat have diarrhea in the morning? Is he also listless, or did he eat food that was a little bit oily the previous evening? If the diarrhea persists for more than a day or two or your cat exhibits other symptoms, have him checked by your veterinarian. Catching a problem early when it is still treatable is one of the best ways to ensure your cat's continued well-being. Between annual checkups, make note of any symptom or behavior that seems suspect from a medical standpoint and discuss it with your veterinarian.

Here are some early warning signs that may indicate that your cat is ill:

- Blood in the stools or urine
- Cessation of self-grooming
- Change in thirst
- Constipation
- Coughing
- Crying for no apparent reason
- Diarrhea for more than a day
- Gagging
- Hair loss
- Lethargy
- Limping
- Loss of appetite
- Nasal discharge
- Scratching excessively
- Sneezing
- Sudden aggression or antisocial behavior
- Tearing or cloudiness in one or both eyes
- Vomiting
- Weight loss or weight gain
- Wheezing

PROFILE:
MAKING A HEALTHY DIFFERENCE
IN SAN FRANCISCO

Mousie was twenty years old when she came to the San Francisco SPCA via the city's Animal Control Center. She suffered from kidney ailments and low potassium, and she required a special diet to reduce the risk of contracting further problems. May May had a cold, an eye infection, a skin allergy and an upset stomach when she arrived at the SF/SPCA. Aida had a sore eye that had to be removed. Moon Doggy was diagnosed with diabetes and required daily insulin.

While other shelters might have considered these animals beyond hope and unadoptable, the SF/SPCA gave them veterinary medical attention at the PeopleSoft Pet Recovery Center, the SF/SPCA's medical unit, which provides veterinary care to stray, abandoned or homeless animals in San Francisco. After treatment, they were offered for adoption by someone willing to care for them in spite of their disabilities.

In 1995, when it became obvious that the SF/SPCA's existing veterinary care unit was not large enough to accommodate the additional animals it obtained via the Adoption Pact or its comprehensive goals for spaying and neutering the city's pets, an expansion provided a new facility with a spacious surgical theater, two treatment areas and fourteen recovery wards. Funded by PeopleSoft, Inc., a software company headquartered in California, the new PeopleSoft Pet Recovery Center treats more than 4,000 animals per year and spays or neuters 9,000 more. Adjacent to the SF/SPCA, the center has a staff of forty-seven people, including veterinarians, technicians, animal behaviorists, surgeons and veterinary assistants.

The Recovery Center gives necessary medical attention to animals retrieved from the SF/SPCA's daily visits to the Animal Control Center as well as any coming directly to the SF/SPCA. Once returned to health, the animals are put up for adoption at the organization's shelter. Through the center, the SF/SPCA

Bubbles had polyps removed from her ear canal and a growth removed from her eyelid by the veterinary staff of the PeopleSoft Pet Recovery Center at the San Francisco SPCA. (Photo courtesy of the San Francisco SPCA.)

continues to provide medical attention to animals that need it after they are adopted. If an adopted cat is diabetic, for example, the SF/SPCA will provide insulin for the rest of the cat's life.

Another of the three medical units run by the SF/SPCA is the SF/SPCA Animal Hospital, a private, client-based, fee-based animal hospital that is accredited by the American Animal Hospital Association, an international association that establishes standards for animal hospitals and pet health care. The hospital treats more than 25,000 pets belonging to Bay Area residents every year. Some services are offered at a lower cost or free to the homeless, seniors or others with limited financial ability to care for their pets.

The SF/SPCA also runs a spay and neuter clinic, where all animals are altered before they are adopted. It periodically pays people living in the city to bring in pets to be spayed or neutered or to round up feral or stray animals for the same purpose.

Forward-thinking organizations such as the SF/SPCA are helping to alleviate animal suffering and making a significant difference in the pet overpopulation problem in the region they serve.

A shelter cat obtains a medical exam at the PeopleSoft Pet Recovery Center. (Photo courtesy of the San Francisco SPCA.)

A charming kitten receives the necessary medical attention at the PeopleSoft Pet Recovery Center. (Photo courtesy of the San Francisco SPCA.)

VIRAL DISEASES

Viruses are a major threat to your cat's good health. Keeping your cat indoors will lessen the chance that he will contract a virus or viral infection, but it is no guarantee. Some viruses remain dormant and have no effect on their host, while others may attack the host's immune system and leave him susceptible to other conditions or illnesses. Viruses do not respond to antibiotics, and if there is no vaccination available to prevent contracting the virus, the only method of treatment is to address secondary symptoms of the disease. In fact, most vaccines prevent cats from succumbing to the full-blown disease but do not prevent initial infection.

Viral diseases for which there are preventive vaccines that are part of your cat's annual checkup were mentioned previously. Vaccines are available to treat some of the conditions that follow, but your veterinarian will not administer them to your cat unless you give permission.

Feline Leukemia Virus

One of the diseases that has received considerable attention in recent years is *feline leukemia virus* (FeLV). First discovered in the mid-1960s, FeLV is a contagious disease transmitted via an infected cat's saliva through bite wounds, mutual grooming, communal food bowls, litter boxes and in utero from a mother cat to her kittens.

Feline leukemia virus is not airborne, so your cat will have to come into direct contact with an FeLV-positive cat in order to catch it. About 30 percent of the cats that come into contact with the virus develop an immunity and simply shed the virus. The other 70 percent either become carriers and therefore are capable of infecting other cats they come into contact with, or they succumb to the disease. Latent carriers can live normal lives, and they may show no visible signs of the disease but can pass it on to offspring. Preventing transmission of such diseases is another great reason to spay or neuter your cat.

Feline leukemia virus produces different symptoms in different cats. The most common symptoms are poor coat, loss of weight and wasting, and anemia visible as pale gums. Cats with FeLV may develop tumors or anemia, exhibit neurological problems, lose their blood-clotting ability or suffer from complete suppression of their immune system. FeLV-positive cats may live from one to three years.

Your veterinarian will be able to test your cat to determine if he has FeLV. The shelter from which you adopted him may have already tested him, in which case you will simply need to discuss with your veterinarian whether you want to have your cat vaccinated. No cure exists for feline leukemia virus, so vaccination is the only way to prevent your cat from contracting the disease. Several types of vaccines exist, and your veterinarian will be able to recommend one to you. Again, keeping your cat indoors will reduce his risk of exposure. But to be safe, have him vaccinated against FeLV.

Feline Infectious Peritonitis

Feline infectious peritonitis (FIP) also was first diagnosed in the mid-1960s. The FIP virus affects the white blood cells that are an important part of a cat's immune system and transport the virus to other parts of the body.

There are two types of FIP: a wet type (the cat develops fluid buildup and presents a pot-bellied appearance) and a dry form.

Feline infectious peritonitis can cause a broad range of conditions, from no symptoms at all to full-blown FIP. The most common symptoms are recurring fevers of unknown origins and sporadic, intermittent diarrhea.

Feline infectious peritonitis is most often found in cats under four years old, but it can affect cats of any age. Although it is less common than FeLV, it is a serious condition. Scientists are not sure how FIP is transmitted but suspect that the virus is either ingested or inhaled. Cats suffering from FIP might show signs of loss of appetite, depression, weight loss and fever. One of the most common symptoms of FIP is the accumulation of fluid and swelling of the abdomen. Although tests exist to determine if a cat has FIP, they are not conclusive. FIP is fatal, so a cat that has contracted FIP will be expected to die within a few months of when the symptoms become visible.

Serums against FIP have been produced, but the veterinary community questions whether their use is appropriate. The best candidate for use of the serum would be a cat that lives outdoors or in a multi-cat household with other cats that have the disease.

Feline Immunodeficiency Virus

Feline immunodeficiency virus (FIV) was first discovered in the 1980s in a feral cat colony in California. It is a virus that attacks a cat's immune system and leaves him unable to fight off infection or disease. Symptoms of FIV are difficult to isolate, because they may involve secondary conditions contracted because of FIV. The most common symptom is gingivitis (inflammation of the gums), and a cat with FIV may have recurring fevers. The presence of gingivitis or a fever in your cat does not mean that he has contracted FIV. Many cats that have FeLV also carry FIV.

No vaccination exists to prevent FIV. The best prevention is to keep your cat away from infected cats. Once a cat is infected, treatment serves to fight the secondary conditions that arise. Indoor cats are unlikely to contract FIV. A test exists to detect FIV, so if your cat appears to chronically come down with illnesses, discuss having the test administered. Typically, if your veterinarian tests your cat for FeLV, he or she will test for FIV at the same time.

Cats with FIV are often described as having feline AIDS (auto-immune deficiency syndrome). FIV is part of the same family of viruses that causes AIDS in humans and similar conditions in sheep and horses, but FIV is not a *zoonotic* disease, and therefore it cannot be transmitted from a cat to another species. FIV is not AIDS, and you cannot get AIDS from your cat, nor can a person with AIDS give the disease to a cat.

As mentioned in previous chapters, if you are bringing a new shelter cat into a household with other cats, isolate him until he is tested for these contagious diseases. If you get a confirmed diagnosis, you should isolate your cat permanently to prevent the spread of the disease to your other cats.

WHEN YOUR CAT IS SICK

Hopefully, with all of the good care and preventive medicine you practice with your feline companion, you will seldom have to face illness in your pet. Considering how long cats live, however, it is likely that you will have to manage a health problem a few times during your cat's life.

Pill-Popping Time

If your cat gets sick, you will be required to give him medicine. Cats accept or refuse being medicated to varying degrees, and there is no way to tell how your cat will respond until you must proceed with the dreaded deed. Even a cat that has been laying around ill and listless and perhaps weakened from loss of appetite can find the strength of Hercules to resist opening his mouth so that you can insert a pill or dropper full of antibiotic pink stuff into it.

The pilling method most often recommended is to place one hand over your cat's head. With your other hand, open his mouth and insert the pill, making sure to push it as far back into his mouth as possible. Some cats are quite devious in their utter rejection of medication, so that it may seem as if your cat has consumed it when, in reality, he's simply waiting to spit it out later when you're not looking. Cat owners can find it very frustrating to find partially dissolved pills on the floor when they assumed that they had been successful in medicating their pet.

The more skillful at the pilling process you become, the better off your cat will be. Because pilling can become a stressful process for cat owners as well as their cats, well-developed pilling skills will serve you both.

To help restrain your cat, especially if you have no one who can help you with this process, kneel on the floor and place your cat between your legs with his front end facing outward. Gently hold him between your legs while you administer the medication.

Other methods of keeping Kitty secure are wrapping him in a towel or pillowcase with only his head exposed. Manufacturers have introduced a product resembling a bag with drawstring handles in which to stuff Kitty at pill time. The bag functions as a feline straightjacket and helps keep the cat calm while being medicated.

Some cat owners resort to trickery to entice their cats to take medication. Because it is so important to get the medicine into a sick cat, don't feel the least bit guilty about resorting to methods such as inserting the pill into a moist cat treat, covering it with butter, grinding it up and mixing it with wet cat food, mixing it with a hairball remedy or mixing a liquid medicine in the juice from canned tuna packed in water.

You might also want to check out a device called a *pill gun* available at pet stores or from veterinarians. Pill guns look somewhat like a syringe. You place the pill into a soft, rubberized tip, insert the gun into your cat's mouth and shoot the pill into it. Pill guns require a bit of manual dexterity, but if your cat is putting up a fight when it comes to pill-popping time, anything that will work will benefit both of you.

Medicines come in different forms, so if you are having trouble getting pills into your cat, discuss other options, such as liquid medicine, with your veterinarian.

The Sick Room

When your cat becomes ill and needs to recover, it is important to provide him with a space in which he can have some privacy as well as peace of mind to ensure that the healing process takes place. While he is recovering, put him in a room away from the noise and hubbub of the household or other animals living in it. Provide him with all the essentials that he will need—food, water, litter box and bed. Because he is sick, your cat probably will not want to play, so having toys available will not be necessary.

If your cat is not grooming himself as much as usual, gently brush and comb him. Spend as much time with him as possible. Continued contact with you, his caregiver, will be important in his recovery. Give him whatever he wants to eat. Sick cats frequently lose their appetites, so it is important that they eat whatever they can. If your cat is not eating as much as he usually does, offer him some baby food in turkey, chicken or beef flavors to entice him to eat.

If you have other cats in the household, it is important for their well-being to isolate a sick cat. Cats that share food and water bowls, litter boxes and scratch posts and that engage in mutual grooming clearly risk contracting any contagious disease from an infected animal.

EMERGENCY FIRST AID

If you have cat-proofed your home as recommended in Chapter 5, "Bringing Home Baby," you have taken the first steps to helping prevent emergencies and accidents from befalling your cat. If you will keep your shelter cat indoors, your cat will not run the risk of being hit by a car, attacked by a wild animal, abused by others, or caught in any type of trap intended for wild animals. As careful as you can be as a cat owner, however, no home environment is 100-percent safe or free of potential hazards, so knowing how to respond to emergencies may help save your cat's life if he is placed in a life-threatening situation.

Recognizing an emergency is the first step. Obviously, if your cat coughs once, it is not an emergency, but if your cat appears not to be able to breathe due to incessant coughing, you have an emergency on your hands. If your cat is bleeding, choking, experiencing convulsions, is paralyzed or in shock, repeatedly vomits or gags or is unable to urinate, you must obtain emergency care immediately.

You should know how your veterinarian addresses emergencies. Will he or she take after-hours, weekend or holiday calls, or will you be referred to an emergency clinic if the practice is not open at the time of the emergency? Keep all necessary telephone numbers handy so that you can obtain the services your cat needs at any hour of the day or night.

Don't wait until an emergency happens to become familiar with the procedures for handling one. If you have an emergency, you will need to respond quickly and effectively. Your cat's life may depend on it.

If an accident happens, remain calm. Check your cat's vital signs. Is he breathing? What is his heart rate? A healthy cat's heart beats approximately 140 to 260 beats per minute. He takes twenty to thirty breaths per minute. His temperature will be 100.2 to 102.4 degrees. Make note of his heart and respiratory rate and his temperature for your veterinarian. Check the color of your cat's mucous membranes. The gums should be pink. Put pressure on them with your finger and release. The pressure point should be white but return to pink. If the cat is in shock, the gums will stay pale where you pressed. When you contact your veterinarian or emergency clinic, describe what happened and your cat's symptoms.

Make a first-aid kit and keep it handy. A first-aid kit should contain the following materials:

- Activated charcoal tablets (for absorbing ingested poisons)
- Antibacterial ointment for the eyes and skin
- Cat shampoo to wash off topical poison
- A cat muzzle, because many cats become aggressive when injured or in pain
- Cotton swabs
- Milk of magnesia tablets
- Nonstick wound pads in various sizes
- One-inch and two-inch rolls of gauze bandages
- A one-inch roll of adhesive tape
- A rectal thermometer
- Rubbing alcohol
- Scissors
- Sterile cotton balls

- A styptic pencil (a short, medicated stick applied to a cut to slow or stop bleeding)
- Three-by-three-inch gauze pads
- Three-percent hydrogen peroxide
- Triangular bandages
- Tweezers

Once you have used the materials, replace them so that you can have a supply on hand if another emergency arises.

Bleeding

Like humans, cats bleed externally and internally; obviously, internal bleeding is more difficult to detect. Internal bleeding is not always an emergency. If you notice blood in your cat's stools or urine, for example, you should seek veterinary care as soon as possible, but it is not an emergency situation. If you are in doubt, contact your veterinarian and describe the symptoms you observe. If you notice blood leaking from your cat's mouth or anal area, it may be a sign that he has been injured internally. Control the situation by making sure that nothing is obstructing his air passages, treating him for shock or immobilizing him in case of broken bones. Such a situation requires that you get your cat to a veterinarian as soon as possible (see "Stabilizing and Transporting an Injured Cat," below, for more information).

External bleeding, if it does not stop in a few minutes, requires immediate attention while you enlist the care of your veterinarian or emergency clinic. External bleeding can be caused by lacerations, puncture wounds or abrasions. Lacerations and puncture wounds are the most dangerous and life-threatening conditions. If you are not able to stop the bleeding, your cat could bleed to death. Firmly applying a pressure bandage is the best way to stop the bleeding until you can get your cat to the veterinarian. Depending on the wound, use a roll of gauze bandage or apply a nonstick pad and wrap gauze around it to keep it secure. Do not apply a tourniquet unless absolutely necessary and only at the direction of a veterinarian.

If your cat experiences a scrape or abrasion, clip the hair around the wound. Clean the area with an antiseptic such as hydrogen peroxide or alcohol on a cotton swab or gauze pad. Cover the wound with a sterile gauze pad or gauze bandage until it can be examined by a veterinarian.

Burns

Burns occur most often when a cat has jumped onto a hot surface or singed his hair by the flame of a candle. These burns are called *thermal* burns. *Electrical* burns occur if a cat chews into a power cord, and *chemical* burns result from contact with poisons. Good pet-proofing will help prevent such accidents from befalling your cat.

If your cat experiences a thermal burn, wash the area with cold water. Never apply an ointment or butter to a burn area. If the burn covers large areas of the cat's body or appears to be deeper than skin level, seek emergency treatment.

If your cat experiences electrical burns, first turn off the source of the power. Electrical burns will cause damage to the cat's mouth and surrounding skin. An electrical shock can cause convulsions, unconsciousness or loss of pulse. If your cat is still attached to the electrical cord, remove him and listen for a heartbeat if he is motionless. Often, electrical burns will cause the cat to go into shock, and you may need to administer artificial respiration.

First, open the cat's mouth and extend his tongue. Extend the cat's head and neck. Make sure that the cat's airways are not blocked. Close the cat's mouth and place your mouth over his nose and exhale. When the cat's lungs inflate, wait for them to relax again before repeating the process. Repeat the inflation and deflation process up to twenty-four times per minute.

Chemical burns can result from your cat coming into contact with poisons. Household cleaning products, drain openers, car batteries, rodent poisons, snail bait, antifreeze, herbicides, insecticides, plant food, some types of houseplants, paints, human medicines, lighter fluid, household disinfectants and some foods such as chocolate pose life-threatening hazards to your cat if he comes into contact with or ingests them. If the poisoning is topical, bathe your cat with a cat shampoo to remove the poison.

If your cat comes into contact with or ingests a poisonous substance, he may experience convulsions; show signs of white, gray or black burns; vomit or experience respiratory distress. Treatment for poisons vary, depending on the type and nature of the substance. Before administering any medication, contact your veterinarian or the poison-control center in your area. If you are unable to reach them, call the National Animal Poison Information Center at 800-548-2423. If you are calling the for first time about a new case, the center will charge you $30.00, so keep your credit card handy. If it is poisoning due to a product that your cat ingested, you might be able to recoup the cost from the product manufacturer later.

Before calling a poison help center, try to determine what poison your cat came into contact with. It will aid in helping the center tell you what to do to minimize the situation. Never give a cat over-the-counter medicine that contains acetaminophen (the active ingredient in Tylenol™), ibuprofen or aspirin. Such remedies are toxic to cats.

Choking

Cats will choke on any small object that becomes lodged in their throats. Small bells or parts from unsafe toys, sewing needles or pins, tin foil, and soda-bottle tops are just some of the dangerous objects your cat may think are fun to play with and inadvertently swallow. Once the object is stuck, your cat will gag and try to dislodge it. He may show signs of labored breathing and paw at his mouth.

If your cat appears to be choking, open his mouth and see if the object is visible. If it is obstructing his airways, he may not be able to breath. If possible, reach into his mouth to retrieve the item. If you can't reach the obstructing item, grab your cat just under the ribcage, tip his nose downward and give him a quick squeeze. Or, place him on his side. Placing one hand on his spine, push down and forward behind his ribcage several times. If the object does not come out, or if he continues to have difficulty breathing, obtain veterinary care immediately. If the object does come out, contact your veterinarian to have the cat examined to ensure that it did not cause any internal injuries.

Stabilizing and Transporting an Injured Cat

Injured cats are often frantic and may not recognize their owners. If your cat is injured, he may be in pain and afraid and will not necessarily understand that you are trying to help him. As a result, he may lash out or bite when you try to restrain him. However, keeping him calm and stationary will be an important part of emergency care. If he has a broken bone or internal injuries, you will want to make sure that he does not move around and make the injury worse.

If your injured cat is thrashing, secure his front legs and wrap some one-inch gauze gently but firmly around them to hold them in place. Secure the hind legs in a similar manner. Immobilizing your cat will help you examine him if you must look in his mouth or treat a wound.

Under these circumstances, it is important that you talk to your cat and reassure him. Slip a pillowcase, blanket or towel under him and place him gently into a sturdy cat carrier. You may have to remove the top of the carrier to lift him into it without risking further injury. If the cat appears to be frightened or struggling, cover his body with a blanket or towel, leaving his head exposed, and place another one over the carrier openings to help calm him. Get your cat to your veterinarian or an emergency clinic as soon as possible.

Inability to Urinate

An obstruction of the urethra resulting in an inability to urinate is an emergency. If not addressed immediately, it can cause your cat's bladder to rupture. The cause of *feline lower urinary tract disorder* (FLUTD) is unknown. It results in the inflammation of the bladder or urethra or in the formation of stones that cause obstruction. Signs of this condition include urinating small and frequent amounts, crying when urinating, excessive licking of the anal area and bloody urine.

If the stones block the urethra, they will cause difficulty in urination or inability to urinate altogether. If your cat makes repeated trips to the litter box but fails to urinate, have him treated immediately by your veterinarian.

WHAT'S OLD IS NEW

In recent years, people have begun to seek out and explore alternative methods of dealing with illnesses beyond contemporary allopathic medicine. Instead of treating symptoms of a disease, alternative medicine, often referred to as *holistic medicine,* tries to treat the whole person (or, in this case, animal), not just an individual symptom of his illness. With today's increased emphasis on preventive medicine and the relationship of things like diet to the overall health of a person or animal, most doctors and veterinarians, whether they practice holistic or allopathic medicine or a combination of both, are looking at the total being to find causes for diseased states of health. They will investigate issues in addition to the immediate problem occurring in the patient's body and will explore ways in which the patient's environment may be contributing to the problem.

Alternative medicine has found its way into veterinary medical practice as well as human medicine. Veterinary medical colleges are beginning to teach their students these alternative forms of treatment and therapy, many of which were first used hundreds or even thousands of years ago.

Alternative veterinary care can be used by itself or in conjunction with contemporary treatments such as vaccinations and surgery. Holistic medicine that is often used by veterinarians can include herbal medicine, homeopathy, acupuncture, chiropractic, massage and TTouch. Very often, holistic treatments can help to heal an animal when no contemporary treatment is available. They can also facilitate healing when the side effects of a treatment are undesirable or when the problem is behavioral. Holistic treatments are intended to strengthen the animal's body and help him use his natural defense systems to promote healing.

If you are interested in finding a veterinarian who practices holistic medicine, contact the American Holistic Veterinary Medical Association (see Chapter 10, "Resources"). Many veterinarians use holistic techniques as a part of a total health-care program that includes diet and nutritional counseling.

Homeopathy

Imagine giving your cat medicine to cure an ailment that in higher doses causes the same symptoms as those the sick pet is exhibiting. Imagine that the names for those treatments look like they came from a guidebook to an exotic garden or a field of mineral deposits. Such is the technique a homeopathic veterinarian uses to treat animals—the same treatment (or *remedy*, as it is called in homeopathic medicine) that causes an illness or symptom to occur cures the condition. The remedies have names like *belladonna, echinacea, lycopodium, hepar sulphuris, silicea,* and *nux vomica.*

Veterinarians prescribe homeopathic remedies in the smallest possible dilution, depending on the nature of the problem or illness. The remedy is given only until the symptom subsides. If a new symptom appears, the animal is treated with a different remedy until he is restored to complete health.

Homeopathic remedies are prepared in a very specific way by diluting the substance gleaned from its natural plant or mineral source, progressively diluting it and vigorously shaking it. How homeopathic remedies work is unclear. The veterinary and scientific communities have only begun to put homeopathic remedies through their clinical paces, but pet owners who have had their pets treated by homeopathic veterinarians swear that their pets get well as a result of the treatments.

PROFILE:
ALTERNATIVE THERAPIES ACHIEVE SUCCESS

After Tree House Animal Foundation, Inc.'s feline behavioral specialist Sandra Newbury consulted with a homeopathic veterinarian for her own cats, she began to wonder how the shelter cats might respond to homeopathic treatments. A brown tabby kitten named Jessy had come to Tree House having succumbed to an epidemic of feline distemper that had hit Chicago. Not only did Jessy have distemper, but he also suffered from mouth ulcers and diarrhea. He was unable to eat and was lethargic and unresponsive in his cage in the isolation area. His prognosis was not good.

After consulting with her homeopathic veterinarian and obtaining permission from the Tree House management and medical personnel, Newbury tried the remedy Baptisia on the kitten. The next morning, Jessy was up and jumping around in his cage. His mouth, which had exhibited ulceration and inflammation, was healed. At that point, the Tree House Treatment Center drew blood and discovered that the kitten's white blood count had risen from his previous 3,300 to over 26,000. At that point, Newbury knew that Jessy was fighting back. His blood count became normal over the next several days, and his symptoms never returned.

Tree House Animal Foundation, Inc. uses homeopathic treatments as part of a total veterinary program that also includes traditional allopathic medicine, such as vaccinations, surgery and pharmacological drugs to restore an animal to health. Thanks to the generosity of Newbury's homeopathic veterinarian, Lynda Clark, D.V.M., and a donation to the shelter, Tree House is achieving great results using homeopathy as an additional treatment for pet patients who could benefit from it.

Tree House Animal Foundation was founded in 1971. This no-kill, cageless shelter is located in Chicago, Illinois. Tree House operates a veterinary medical facility and an adoption center. The organization offers animal-rescue services, foster-care programs, a pet-food pantry for owners who can't afford to feed their pets and an animal information and behavior hot line,. It also provides early and low-cost spay and neuter services and pet-assisted therapy.

Herbal Medicine

One of the oldest forms of medical treatments is herbal medicine. The use of herbs to cure illnesses dates back thousands of years to when early man consumed certain types of plants to enhance his sense of well-being. Herbs are derived from plant, animal and mineral sources, and their uses have been handed down from generation to generation as a traditional form of folk medicine. In fact, some types of contemporary medications have their roots in herbal medicine, such as the heart medicine digitalis, which is made from the foxglove plant.

Herbal medicine is becoming increasingly popular as a method of treating pets. Interest has been growing in traditional Chinese herbs as well as those found in the West. Herbs are used to treat diverse conditions, such as internal and external parasites, mange, constipation and colds. These herbs can be used with allopathic medical treatments and therapies. As with homeopathy, diagnosis of the correct herbal treatment is best performed by a veterinarian trained in the technique of using herbs to solve a medical problem.

Veterinary Acupuncture

Acupuncture is a system of healing that was developed thousands of years ago by the Chinese. When an animal is healthy, his energy or life force, called *chi* by the Chinese, flows along well-defined channels in the skin called *meridians*. The meridians are connected to the animal's internal organs, muscles and nervous system. When the animal is sick, it causes an imbalance in the positive energy flow, which can be corrected by stimulating points along the meridians with tiny acupuncture needles. Acupuncture is often used on animals to alleviate pain or to address medical problems such as arthritis, although it is used to treat other conditions as well. Acupuncture can be used with acupressure and massage therapies.

Acupuncture is recognized as a valid therapy by the American Veterinary Medical Association. Veterinarians who practice acupuncture receive training and certification through the International Veterinary Acupuncture Society (IVAS). To contact them for a list of certified veterinary acupuncturists, see Chapter 10, "Resources."

VETERINARY INSURANCE

As a pet owner, you will never know what illnesses or accidents might occur during the life of your cat. To help pet owners manage the costs of unforeseen health problems, veterinary insurance providers have become increasingly available in recent years. Depending on the nature and severity of the health problem, veterinary costs to treat it can run in the hundreds or even thousands of dollars.

Like health insurance for people, pet owners pay a premium that may change with the age of the pet. There are medical costs that are covered and those that are not, depending on the insurance provider. Most plans, however, apply only to sudden or traumatic illnesses or accidents and do not cover ongoing, preventive care. Some pet-insurance plans also include added features, such as pet-identification tags and membership in a nationwide lost pet network.

If you are interested in obtaining a veterinary insurance plan for your cat, discuss the options with your veterinarian. Make sure that you understand the extent of the coverage. For example, does the plan cover routine office visits and vaccinations, or does it only cover extra-ordinary costs such as surgery, referral to specialists and long-term treatments? Your veterinarian may be able to recommend a plan to you.

BUDGETING FOR HEALTH CARE

If you choose not to enroll in a veterinary health-insurance plan, there are other ways in which you can help cover veterinary costs that are effective and painless.

Discuss obtaining credit with your veterinarian in the event that a sudden, unexpected problem arises. Many veterinarians will work out payment arrangements with good customers who would rather see their cats obtain treatment than euthanize them because of lack of funds. The key word here is *good* customers. Don't take advantage of your veterinarian for ongoing costs, or you may find that when you need it most, leniency in the payment department is unavailable to you.

Your veterinarian may agree to have you pay a fixed amount each month that is credited toward your cat's routine care. Five or ten dollars every month or so will add up and can be used for any expense you might incur with your veterinarian.

If you prefer to put money aside and keep the interest yourself, think about starting a small savings account that will enable you to save for your cat's rainy day.

GOOD NUTRITION

Good nutrition that is formulated for the age of your cat will play an integral part in your cat's overall health. Proper diet, along with plenty of exercise and mental stimulation, will go a long way toward ensuring your cat's continued well-being.

Visit any grocery store or supermarket, and you'll find that the pet food occupies one entire aisle. Shop in a pet superstore, and you'll discover even more selections from which to choose. You'll see kitten food; food for adult and senior cats; food for tubby tabbies and food developed to treat specific health conditions, such as kidney problems, lower urinary tract blockage or allergies. Given all of the choices, deciding which food to select for your cat can be complicated.

To compound the issue, your cat may decide to devour his breakfast and turn his nose up at the same food fed to him in the evening. Cats have a reputation for being finicky, and no matter how long you labor reading cat-food labels to pick what's best for Buster, Buster may have his own ideas about what he wants. So, don't commit yourself to any one particular type or brand of cat food. Experiment a little to see that his food meets not only his nutritional requirements but his personal tastes as well. Giving your cat a variety of foods that include a few different flavors will be sure to please him as well as contribute to his overall health and happiness.

Pet stores carry a selection of premium cat food for all the stages of your cat's life. (Photo courtesy of Karen Commings.)

Your cat is likely to want just about any kind of food that seems tasty from his point of view. It may be tasty from your point of view, too, which is why your cat may want to participate in your meals as much as his own. Cats have been known to look at all sorts of foods as gastronomic delights, so don't be surprised if your cat wants to partake of your spaghetti, yogurt, spinach, chili or cantaloupe in addition to your roast beef, baked chicken or tuna casserole. It's okay to give your cat an occasional treat from the table, but people food should make up less than 15 percent of your cat's total food intake.

Aside from what your cat wants, there are nutrients your cat needs. Any food that you give your cat should be balanced for his needs and should say "complete and balanced nutrition" on the label. It should contain adequate amounts of protein, vitamins, minerals, fats and carbohydrates.

Protein

Cats need protein that has its base in animal products, and unlike dogs, cats cannot live on a vegetarian diet. Protein is the major component of your cat's hair, skin and musculature. Protein in food will provide your cat with energy and the amino acids to build new cells and tissue. Protein in cat food comes from meat, fish, poultry, meat byproducts, liver and bone meal.

Fat

Fat supplies cats with fuel for energy. Fatty deposits around organs and under the skin protect your cat against physical injury. All cats should have some fatty tissue on their bodies. Fat is often added to cat food to make it more appealing to your cat's taste buds. Food that is intended to help a cat lose weight will be lower in fat than other cat food.

Carbohydrates

Carbohydrates include starches and sugars and provide an additional source of energy for your pet. Carbohydrates are not critical to a cat's health but are included in most cat foods. Carbohydrate sources such as grains or cooked potatoes are also a good source of bulk in your cat's diet.

Vitamins and Minerals

Your cat's food should contain an adequate amount of vitamins and minerals. Vitamins are required for growth and maintenance of healthy tissue and bones and for proper metabolism. Minerals also help your cat build body tissue and are essential for your cat's body processes.

Some cat owners feel that they should offer their cats vitamin supplements in addition to their regular meals. If the food you are giving your cat is complete and balanced, extra vitamins are unnecessary and may cause an imbalance. If your cat develops a condition, such as anemia, as he ages, discuss with your veterinarian feeding him supplements.

CAT-FOOD LABELS

The contents of pet foods and how their labels are formatted are regulated by the Association of American Feed Control Officials (AAFCO), a volunteer organization of officials from the departments in state governments that regulate animal feed of all types. AAFCO standardizes animal-feed production procedures and product labeling so that consumers can depend on the food's content and nutritional value.

Manufacturers must include a lot of information on a pet-food label, so you may be carting a magnifying glass along when you shop for cat food. Of course, the brand of the food and its flavor will be right on the front of the label, but the ingredients portion will be on the back or side and in smaller print.

After you take out your magnifying glass and hold it up to the cat-food can, you will usually read a statement such as "Animal feeding tests using AAFCO procedures substantiate that *brand name* provides complete and balanced nutrition for all life stages of cats." The statement may vary slightly, depending on whether the food is intended for kittens, adults or seniors.

The guaranteed analysis section of pet-food labels contains the sources for ingredients listed in the order of each ingredient's percentage of total content, from highest to lowest. Crude protein, crude fat, crude fiber and moisture are listed in decreasing percentages. The term *crude* refers to the method used to estimate the quantity of that ingredient in food. Cat-food labels also must contain the mineral content—such as calcium, salt, phosphorus and taurine—and the food's *ash content*, which is the noncombustible material left in the food after processing.

Following the guaranteed analysis is the ingredients section. Ingredients are listed in order of predominance by weight. In meat production, no part of the animal is wasted. If the label says "meat," it will be from the clean flesh of animals. It can also include tissue from the tongue, the diaphragm, heart or esophagus. *Meat byproducts* are the non-rendered clean parts other than meat, including the blood, brain, stomach, intestines and other organs but not the hair, hooves, bones or ears. *Meat meal* consists of unidentified renderings from the processing plant and can include whatever the plant has at the time. If the food has bone in it, the label must say "meat and bone meal." Meat meal is ground into a powder.

Poultry byproducts are the leftover parts that humans don't eat, such as heads, feet and viscera. They must be free from fecal contents and foreign matter. *Poultry meal* is the dry meal from grinding clean flesh and skin (with or without bone) into a powder. It must be free of feathers, heads, feet and entrails. If a cat-food label says "chicken or chicken byproducts," it must be chicken and not turkey or vice versa. Manufacturers can also use fish and fish meal in the same way in cat foods. Fish oil is often added to enhance flavor.

Manufacturers add ingredients to pet food that may or may not be nutritionally required. Ground corn or corn gluten meal, wheat flour, rice and soy are added as fillers or to add fiber to the food, which is important to a cat's health. Additives that are nutritional include vitamins, minerals, fats and amino acids. Other additives enhance the color, flavor and aroma and are intended to make the food more palatable to pets.

The U.S. Department of Agriculture must approve any artificial color that is added. Because of health problems created by the addition of certain colors to pet food, some manufacturers of commercial food are eliminating it from their products. Artificial color is designed to appeal to the cat owner rather than the cat, which may not be able to perceive the color, so buying food with no color added will not make a difference in how much your cat wants to eat it. Premium pet food and foods developed to treat dietary-related health problems do not contain artificial color.

Preservatives are added to food to lengthen its shelf life. Antioxidants, which are found naturally in grains and oils, prevent food from oxidizing and therefore spoiling. Vitamins E and C are natural antioxidants. Preservatives can be synthetic, such as *butylated hydroxyanisole* (BHA) and *butylated hydroxytoluene* (BHT).

Wet, Moist or Dry

When selecting food for your cat, variety is the spice of life. Your cat can exist solely on one type of food, but feeding him several types of cat food will keep him stimulated and interested in his meals as well as provide him with nutrition from several different sources.

Cat food comes in wet (canned), moist and dry varieties. Canned food comes in several sizes. Large cans are generally less expensive per ounce than the smaller cans, but you will have leftovers that must be refrigerated and preferably warmed up again, at least to room temperature, for Kitty's next meal. If you feed your cat cold food, you may find him walking away from his second or third serving from the same can. If left to warm up on its own, you may find it spoiled, depending on the temperature of the room. Of course, you have the choice of nuking the food in the microwave for a few seconds to make it appealing to Kitty's palate. For the person who has only one or two cats, the smaller size cans have their advantages.

Canned food, with its many varieties of flavor, offers you the opportunity to provide protein from several different sources, such as meat, poultry and fish. Good-quality canned cat food, particularly the meat or poultry flavor, does not usually have as offensive an odor as some of the less-costly varieties. Canned cat food contains as much as 75 percent water, which is a necessary part of a cat's diet. The water present in canned cat food, along with a supply of fresh water to drink, will provide your pet with adequate water.

Semi-moist cat food comes in pouches or cardboard containers. As a cat owner, you may find the odor of semi-moist cat food more appealing and the single-serving containers more convenient, but semi-moist cat food contains more additives to keep it fresh than food that is sealed in a can.

Dry food is less expensive than canned or semi-moist cat food and can be left exposed to the air for longer periods of time without deterioration. Chewing dry cat food also helps a cat reduce the buildup of tartar on his teeth. Dry food, however, has a higher magnesium and lower water content and may contribute to the development of a *lower urinary tract disorder* (LUTD). Cats fed solely dry food should be monitored closely to make sure that LUTD does not develop, and they should be given extra amounts of water to drink.

An ideal diet for your cat should include some wet and some dry food in appropriate quantities. Cat-food manufacturers recommend on the product labels the quantity in which their foods should be given, but often it is more than a cat will need, especially if you are using both wet and dry food. Quantities also vary, depending on the size of your cat. Your cat should neither be too thin nor too fat. You should be able to feel your cat's ribs when you pet him, but the ribs should not show through his hair. Experiment to see how much your cat consumes as a meal and discuss appropriate quantities with your veterinarian.

LIFE STAGES

As your cat grows from kitten through adulthood to senior, his dietary needs will change. Providing food for the growth stages of his life will be one of your responsibilities as his caregiver.

Kittens

Your active, growing kitten will have a higher need for energy and body-building foods than an adult or senior cat. Kittens need food with a higher protein content to meet their needs for growth and replacement of tissue. The protein source should contain all of the essential amino acids, including adequate amounts of taurine, which if not present, can result in heart disease or blindness.

When shopping for food, check the label. It should say that it is guaranteed to meet the nutrient requirements for the growing kitten. Kitten food should contain about 30 percent protein and 15 percent fat. Protein should come from high-quality sources, such as meat, meat byproducts, liver and poultry. For your kitten, it's best to allow free feeding by leaving food out for him all of the time to ensure that he gets enough to meet his needs.

Once your cat has been weaned, he will no longer need to be given milk. In fact, for many cats, milk is a source of dietary allergies and produces stomach upset and diarrhea.

Adults

Your cat's needs for growth food will diminish as he becomes an adult. He still will need adequate quantities of protein, fats and other nutrients, but his calorie requirements will be lower than those of a kitten.

To keep your adult cat from becoming overweight, it's best to get him on a regular, twice-daily feeding schedule in which you feed him quantities of food that he can consume within twenty minutes, removing any that he has not consumed. The twenty-minute time period will help you determine how much to feed at each meal.

Seniors

Cats require fewer calories to maintain their energy levels as they age. Due to reduced activity levels, an older cat should be fed cat food with reduced calorie content or reduced quantities of food. An older cat may develop health conditions, such as kidney problems or urinary tract problems, that require special foods designed to help him cope with his condition. Discuss with your veterinarian the needs of your special older cat.

DIGESTIVE UPSETS

As mentioned earlier in this chapter, vomiting and diarrhea are signs that your cat may be ill. They also may be signs that the type of food you are feeding your cat does not agree with his digestive system or that he ate something that he should not have. Food that may be too high in added oils or too fishy may cause him to vomit it back up again shortly after he has eaten or may cause his stools to become loose when he defecates. Giving your cat milk (which he does not need once he's been weaned) may also cause him to have an upset stomach or problems with loose stools.

If you decide to change your cat's diet for one reason or another, do it gradually. Sudden changes in the food you feed your cat can cause digestive upsets. If you suspect that something in your cat's diet is causing him to have digestive problems, bring your concern to your veterinarian. Then, gradually eliminate one food or another to see if the condition subsides. If it does, you can simply remove the offending food from your cat's diet.

YOUR CAT'S MENTAL HEALTH

In addition to ensuring your cat's continued physical health and well-being, you will be responsible for his mental health. Cats do get bored if they are forced to spend their days doing nothing but sleeping or trying to amuse themselves. In addition to needing plenty of hugs and kisses from you, your cat will need you to help him keep mentally alert, stimulated and enjoying life in your home. Boredom, listlessness and neglect often precipitate physical illness, so your continued time and attention will go a long way toward keeping your cat physically as well as mentally healthy. Activities that promote his mental and emotional growth will provide a source of enrichment in his life and help him use his natural instincts and hone his feline skills.

Games

Although today's cat was never a wild animal, cats do retain some of the instincts of their wild ancestors. Feral cats coming to shelters were forced to live their lives as wild animals, using their instincts to survive. When you consider that the domestic cat that is forced to live outdoors is really in an unnatural setting, it becomes doubly cruel to allow your cat to roam freely.

You will learn very quickly after adopting your shelter cat, regardless of his background, that inventing games is a favorite pastime, especially if your cat is young. Ambushing, teasing and pouncing on toys is a way that cats find an outlet for developing their hunting skills and desire to attack prey. Crouching behind an object and lunging at you or another household pet when you or the pet pass by is a way your cat develops his ability to perform a sneak attack on what in the wild may be a potential dinner.

Not all games involve hunting, however, and you may find your cat being very creative in the games that he invents to keep him (and you) occupied. Your cat may hide behind objects until you "find" him as a way of playing hide-and-seek. Your cat also may enjoy finding his own objects that become play things for him. A way to help him in this effort is to hide some of his toys around the house for him to find while you are away or at work. Place the toys under cushions, on shelves or in any other place you think your cat may investigate.

Play and Exercise

Play satisfies a cat's need for mental stimulation and exercise. Baby animals playing with objects in their environment, with their mothers or with each other, are a joy to watch. Play also helps animals develop their instinctive behaviors and prepare for lives as adults.

Providing your cat with toys for him to play with is only half the battle in making sure that he gets enough exercise and play stimulation. As his caregiver, you will need to set aside a time during the day to play with your cat. There are many interactive toys on the market that help keep a cat interested in play and make it easy for you to see that he gets enough exercise:

- A Lucite™ fishing pole with a piece of fabric or a feathers attached to the end of a cord tied to it makes an excellent exercise device. Make sure to put this device away when not in use, however, to prevent your cat from chewing and swallowing the cord.

- A round, plastic track with a Ping-Pong™ ball inside enables your cat to bat at the ball and watch it go around but never leave the track. These track devices are good to have around for your cat to play with when you are not at home.

- A rubber, one-inch ball that you can obtain in a children's store makes a wonderful toy for your cat to chase and bat without hurting himself, you or your belongings.

- A scratch post with toys mounted on springs on the top of it encourage your cat to bat and jump.

BRINGING THE OUTDOORS IN

Most shelters require that adopters keep their cats indoors. The issue of keeping a cat indoors or allowing him to go outside is one that is still hotly debated among cat owners. Animal experts, however, are advising more and more that keeping a cat indoors exclusively is better for the pet than allowing him to roam freely. By keeping your cat indoors, you do the following:

- Prevent him from succumbing to accidents, such as being hit by a car.

- Prevent him from contracting contagious diseases from other cats, such as FeLV, FIV and FIP.

- Prevent him from contracting zoonotic diseases, such as rabies or toxoplasmosis.

- Reduce his risk of contracting parasitic infections, such as from fleas, ticks and various types of worms.

- Prevent him from being attacked by wild animals.

- Prevent him from becoming the victim of pet thieves who resell animals to laboratories, individuals who engage in cruel acts toward cats and other animals and people who place poison in their gardens to get rid of rodents and other pests.

Don't feel that because you are keeping your cat exclusively inside your home that you will be depriving him of his freedom. Freedom is a human concept that is meaningless to your cat. The average life span of a cat that lives in the wild is only about one-third of that of an indoor cat. If you must think in those terms, consider that by keeping your cat inside, he will be free to offer you love, affection and companionship for many more years than he would if you allowed him to roam outside.

Keeping your cat indoors, however, presents some new challenges to you as your cat's caregiver. Cats do have a need for fresh air and sunshine, and they have a need for play and other forms of mental stimulation. You can help your cat get the benefits of outdoor living without the risks by doing some of the following:

- Provide lots of climbing apparatuses for your cat to jump and play on.

- Hang bird and squirrel feeders outside the windows for your cat to watch when they come to feed.

- Attach perches to window sills for your cat to sit on and watch the world outside.

- Although it is a more expensive alternative, build an outdoor run or enclosure and provide access through a pet door. Make sure that the run is safely built to keep your cat from escaping or other neighborhood animals from entering. Another option is to install a secure window enclosure in which your cat can sun himself without going outside.

- Secure your yard with a cat-fencing system to allow him to venture outside but not escape the confines of the yard. Fencing systems are regularly advertised in the national cat magazines (see Chapter 10, "Resources"). Or, contact a local pet store to determine availability.

- Train your cat to go outside on a leash under your supervision. You'll learn more about training in the next chapter, but if you do allow your cat outside on a leash, provide him with shade to avoid the hot sun and plenty of fresh water to drink. Never allow your cat to be tied outside on his own. If he is threatened by another animal, there will be no way for him to escape.

- If you would like to add some additional outdoor excitement to your indoor cat's lifestyle, invest in a video designed to give your cat some outdoor adventure in the comfort and safety of your home. Kitty videos are filled with close-ups of live-action birds, squirrels and fish. Pop one into the VCR and watch your cat's eyes widen as he tries to catch the birds as they fly off the screen or paw at a squirrel that, depending on the size of your television screen, is two or three times bigger than life. Cat videos come complete with sound effects and can be purchased in pet stores or ordered through the Classifieds section at the back of the major cat magazines (see Chapter 10, "Resources").

CHAPTER 7

Basic Training

Look in the Yellow Pages under "Dog Training," and you'll find lots of entries: "Obedience Classes," "Canine Boot Camps," "Private Tutors." Entries under "Cat Training?" I don't think so. As your cat's caregiver, you can expect virtually no professional help in the training department. Even your veterinarian may not be able to offer you much in the way of advice on teaching your cat how to behave and how not to behave. As to modifying your cat's behavior if your training has gone awry or if you are at your wit's end on how to do it— don't count on too much assistance unless your telephone directory has listings under "Applied Animal Behavior Consultants." Not many do, so basically, redirecting your cat's behavior from instinctual to learned may require a willingness on your part to go the distance— even the geographic distance.

Getting your cat off on the right paw in the training department is the first step toward preventing behavior problems later on. Training also will let your cat know what you expect of her—what she *is* supposed to do and what she is *not* supposed to do. Through training, your cat will learn more about you and what will please you. Unlike training a dog, it

151

takes a minimum amount of effort to make a cat easy to live with. You can train your cat to do or *not* do lots of things, but you will have to determine what, beyond a few basic lessons, you will want her to learn.

The first step in training your cat to behave in ways that are appropriate for living indoors with humans is to view things from the cat's perspective. Whenever she acts in a certain way, she is trying to satisfy a basic need. Today's cats have been domesticated for more than 5,000 years, but they still retain a good many of their ancestors' instincts and have an inclination toward what we might want to call *natural* behavior. The domestic cat, while it has never been a wild creature per se, has acquired a good bit of behavioral habits from being forced to live outside as a feral creature for hundreds of years by the very species that domesticated it—man.

The ways in which your cat goes about satisfying her natural urges inside your home as opposed to the world outside may seem to her particularly resourceful and clever. As someone who is about to get caught up in the cat lover's favorite pastime of *cat watching*, you, too, may think they are resourceful and clever, until you come home one day and find your upholstered sofa's innards scattered about the living room. When you begin training your cat or modifying her behavior, remember that she is only trying to find ways to do what comes naturally in what, for her, may be an unnatural environment. Give your cat credit for trying.

CRIME AND PUNISHMENT

Before talking about how to train your cat to do specific things or modifying her behavior to change some things she is doing that you don't care for, a few words about training methods are necessary. Cats do not respond well to negative reinforcement or punishment as a way of learning. Hitting a cat is never a satisfactory way of letting her know that what she has done does not please you. Hitting your cat not only may hurt her physically, but it will destroy her trust in you as her caregiver. If your cat has soiled the carpet, for example, rubbing her nose in it will not tell her that the litter box is the appropriate place to perform her bodily functions. If she has dug up some dirt out of your houseplants while you were at work, yelling at her when you come home will not enable her to associate your reaction with her action.

In all training, whether it is teaching your cat to use the litter box or teaching her to sit up and beg, positive reinforcement is the best method for imparting the lesson. Training requires patience on your part. Give lots of praise when your cat does what you want, even if it is not during a training session; hugs, talking to her in a positive manner and rewards such as food treats are the best ways to let your cat know that what she does pleases you. Because pleasing you is important to your cat, she will learn how to behave in the way you want if the reinforcement for her good behavior is there.

Using discipline is meant to distract your cat from engaging in activities that are unacceptable, such as jumping on the kitchen counter or swinging from a curtain rod. Sometimes distraction is vital, such as when you see your cat about to chomp on an electrical wire. Saying, "Please Kitty, don't do that," may not even attract her attention, much less save her life. At such a moment, you need to be forceful—a simple command like "No" or "Stop," along with a sudden sound such as clapping your hands or snapping your fingers will make your cat pause and teach her that what she is doing at the moment is behavior that you don't appreciate. The key phrase here is *at the moment*. To be an effective learning tool, the sudden surprise must occur when Kitty is in the act of behaving inappropriately. If she has shredded the corner of your favorite easy chair, snapping your fingers an hour or even five minutes later and pointing to the chair won't mean anything to her.

Many cat owners, as well as animal behaviorists, recommend using a squirt bottle or squirt gun to spritz your cat when you must discipline her. The squirt method has some positive and negative aspects to it as a training method. First, when used properly from a respectable but effective distance, a cat will stop what she is doing without associating the discipline method with you. Second, getting a cat a little wet is pretty harmless. The disadvantage to this method is that, in order to be effective, you must catch your cat in the act that you don't want her to engage in. Squirting her two minutes after she has done something that you don't like will be a waste of time. Your cat will not associate being squirted with clawing the corner of your best sofa. Just getting up to run to the kitchen to retrieve the squirt bottle is going to be distracting enough to your cat. That means that you must arm yourself pretty much all the time or keep a squirt bottle handy in virtually every room of the house.

From a practical standpoint, snapping your fingers may be a more effective way to get your cat's attention and distract her from engaging in the inappropriate activity. You are always armed with your fingers, and you'll never have to run to another room looking for them.

When training or disciplining your cat, it is important to remember that what may seem like inappropriate behavior to you is really quite normal in the eyes of your cat. The sofa looks to her like a great place to do her nails. Your cat doesn't know that your sofa cost you hundreds of dollars or that you inherited it from Aunt Emma.

It is only when the behavior becomes inconvenient for life inside the household that it is a problem and must be corrected or redirected. In many cases of feline behavior modification, you will need to offer the cat an alternative (for example, a scratch post for her to do what she needs to do without doing a job on your furniture) or modify your living environment or habits to encourage Kitty to go elsewhere. Solving behavior problems requires careful observation of what your cat is doing and when she is doing it and a willingness to experiment and modify your behavior and environment if necessary. When training your cat or changing her behavior, flexibility is the key.

LITTER-BOX LESSONS

Cats have a natural inclination to dig, so having a litter box full of clean litter will attract an indoor cat like a magnet when she must potty. You might have noticed when you were visiting shelters that some cats stayed in their boxes inside their shelter cages. Why cats at shelters do this is not clear, but the litter box may offer some kind of security for them in an unfamiliar environment. If this is so, your cat may have even more of an attraction to her litter box than her natural desire to dig.

Newborn kittens rely on their mother to teach them a great deal, including how to urinate, which she will do by licking the anal area of the kitten. By the time a cat is six weeks old, she has learned other social behaviors, such as playing, play biting and showing aggression, and how to use the litter box if indoors or how to dig and bury wastes if outdoors. If the mother used a litter box, the kitten would have observed her and imitated her behavior, so knowledge of the kitten's background will help you determine how much effort litter-box training will take on your part. Kittens have been known to drag themselves up into a high-sided litter box that mom uses just to emulate their mother's behavior rather than use the little box meant for them.

One of the first things you should do when you bring your new cat home is show her where the litter box is. Place her in it and say her name so she knows the box belongs to her. If you are isolating your cat so that she can become accustomed to your home gradually, place the litter box in her room, still showing it to her so she makes no mistake about its function.

Adult cats don't lose their knowledge of how to use a litter box but may have substituted burying their wastes in loose soil if they lived outside. So, if your new cat spent time outdoors with her previous owner or was forced to live outside as a stray before coming to the shelter where you adopted her, you may have to refresh her memory by reintroducing her to the box. This situation provides another good reason to confine a new cat to one room of the house initially and introduce her to the rest of the house once she feels comfortable.

Cats typically prefer sand-like clumping litter, but you may have to experiment a little to find one your cat likes. Some litters come with perfume scents added to mask odor, but many cats show an aversion to scented litter. The best way to mask odor is to prevent it by cleaning the box as quickly as possible after Kitty has used it. Common baking soda added to the litter will absorb odors and make the litter box more acceptable to your nose and the nose of your cat. It is also completely safe if your cat gets some on her hair and ingests it when she washes it off.

Litter boxes should be filled with litter to a depth of about three inches. Some cats prefer not to step on litter or have their feet sink into it when they get into the litter box, however. Using lesser amounts or pouring litter into just one end of the box may satisfy your cat if she has an aversion to getting her feet dirty.

Cats often prefer having two litter boxes—one for urinating and one for defecating, so you might try two different kinds of litter, one in each box, to see which one she likes best. Clumping litter tends to be more dust-free than clay litter, so you may prefer it, too. If you have a kitten under two months of age, it's best not to use sand-like litter, because a kitten can ingest it and, given her tiny size, the litter may clog her digestive tract.

If you notice your cat urinating outside of the litter box, have her examined by a veterinarian to make sure the behavior is not caused by a physical problem. If a cat is suffering from a urinary tract blockage, for example, she may try to urinate anywhere she happens to be. So before you assume her actions are behaviorally motivated and invest a lot of time in trying to modify her behavior, take your cat to your veterinarian to make sure that she gets a clean bill of health.

Cat owners occasionally confuse spraying with urinating outside the litter box, but the two actions are quite different. Cats squat to urinate, in or out of the box. Cats spray by backing up against a vertical surface, such as a wall or piece of furniture, while they are standing, lifting their tails and squirting out urine against the vertical surface. Spraying is a way to mark territory. As was discussed earlier, spaying or neutering will eliminate a cat's desire to spray.

Once you've shown your new cat her litter box and she is using it as expected, here are some tips for encouraging her to continue using it:

- Put the box in a clean, dry, convenient place to use.

- Experiment with litter types or brands, if necessary.

- Experiment with the depth of filler in the box.

- Provide two boxes instead of one.

- Experiment with types of litter boxes.

- Provide a litter box that is big enough for the size of your cat.

- Keep the litter box clean by removing waste at least once a day.

- Allow your cat privacy in the potty.

- Don't allow family members to startle your cat or torment her while in the box (or at other times).

- Don't allow family members or other pets to keep her from getting to the litter box.

- If your cat stops using the litter box, here are some questions to ask yourself that may help you determine how to teach her to learn to use it again:

  ❏ Is the box easy to get to and in a convenient place from Kitty's perspective?

  ❏ Is anyone or anything keeping your cat from getting to the box or disturbing her once she is in it?

  ❏ Is the box clean?

  ❏ Is your cat having any health problems, and has she been checked by a veterinarian?

  ❏ Is there any upheaval in the household?

  ❏ Has your cat outgrown her old, small litter box?

  ❏ Is the box covered or automated, and might your cat prefer a simpler or uncovered litter box?

  ❏ Might she prefer a different type of litter?

  ❏ Might she prefer her two litter boxes in different locations?

  ❏ Is your cat's litter box too close to her food and water?

  ❏ Did you try another type of substrate in the bottom of the litter box, such as newspapers, terrycloth towels or one of the newer types of litter made from newspaper pellets or corn husks?

The most common litter-box problem is urinating outside of the box, but occasionally a cat will defecate outside the box, too. Defecating outside the box can be a sign of territorial marking as well, but that is not always the case. If your cat defecates near the box but still outside of it, chances are the box is dissatisfying in some way to your cat. Perhaps it is not clean or your cat does not like your choice of litter. Or, perhaps your cat wants a second box for defecating, and you have not provided one.

Occasionally, a cat will defecate in a sink or tub, which may mean she prefers the smooth surface to that of the litter in her box. If this is the case, using less filler or filler only at one end may encourage your cat to use it. To retrain her, place the box with less filler in the tub or near it and place her in the box when you see her enter the bathroom. Have her examined by a veterinarian to make sure that the problem is not physical.

For all places in your home where your cat has done her business outside of the litter box, clean the soiled area with a cleaner that will soak up odors as well as stains to discourage her from going back to the same place. An enzyme product will work well. Never use an ammonia cleaner on a spot where your cat has urinated. Urine has ammonia in it, and the spot where your cat has urinated will continue to smell like an appropriate place for her to potty.

To further dissuade your cat, place her litter box in the spot where she has urinated or place her food bowls there. As a last resort for a cat that has begun to urinate outside the litter box, confine her to a room with all of her necessities. Once you are sure she has begun to use the litter box again, gradually expand her free range to the rest of your house.

ALL IN THE FAMILY

Aggressive tendencies are some of the most common complaints among cat owners. Cats may show aggression for a variety of reasons. They may be experiencing fear, be sensitive to being touched, be seeking attention or be looking for an outlet for pent-up energy. Regardless of the reason, it can be physically painful when your favorite feline takes a chunk out of your hand or your ankle and emotionally painful, because you were only trying to be nice.

A truly aggressive cat will exhibit unmistakable body language that is intended to scare off the source of her threat. She will flatten her ears, widen her eyes and bare her teeth. She may hiss, spit or even bite. She may scratch or pounce.

A cat inside your home should not experience fear from human or other animal sources, and it is your responsibility to make sure that this does not happen. Cats will generalize, however, from a single bad experience in their past involving one person to people who in the cat's mind are the same or similar. For example, if a cat had a frightening experience with a man, she may find all men frightening. So, if you've brought a loving feline home and discover that she hides under the bed when your boyfriend comes over to meet her, you might have to desensitize her to the experience.

Assure the person in question that your cat's actions are not personal and that, given time, she will learn to like him or her. To that end, your friend should remain patient and not try to force the issue. Never, under any circumstances, pull your cat out of hiding and present her to the person that she is afraid of. That will make her fear the person even more, and she may begin to fear or mistrust you. Allow your cat to stay under the bed or in hiding for several visits from the person. Engage in normal activities that do not involve your cat.

After several visits, allow the person to offer your cat some food treats while still maintaining a respectable distance. The offering of food signals friendship and will begin the process of instilling trust. Have your friend go alone to the room where the cat is hiding, say your cat's name affectionately several times and lay the treats on the floor where she can see and smell them; then leave the room. Do not wait for the cat to come out of hiding to get the treats. This will surprise her and associate another fear with the offering of food. Should that happen, you will have essentially eliminated the potential to use food rewards for future training efforts that may be so important to your life with your cat. Offer food treats in this way on several visits, each time keeping a distance while talking to the cat in a calm voice.

In time, your cat will know that the person is not a threat, and she will begin to come out of hiding to investigate. Being curious by nature, your cat will want to know what's going on when you have visitors, so offering the food treats will reinforce her desire to check things out. When she does come out, allow her to explore the visitor on her own and at her own pace. Again, don't drag your cat over to meet the visitor or allow your visitor to reach for the cat. This will destroy the work that you've done already, and you will have to start over again from square one.

ALL IN FUN

The most common form of aggression experienced by cat owners with their cats is play biting. Cats engage in play biting when they are kittens as a prelude to the more serious type of aggression required to defend

SNAPSHOT:
Cary

One night, a group of young people brought a box and left it at the rear door of Animal Friends, Inc. Inside the box were two cats—a female named Graystoke and a tuxedo cat named Cary. The note attached to the box read:

Dear Friends,

These are Cary (male) and Graystoke (female). The people who lived in the apartment building next to me moved out and left them. They are tame, affectionate, litter trained. It has taken the six of us three weeks of feeding to catch them, but none of us can keep them. They are supposed to be littermates and are six to seven months old. We didn't know what else to do. Please find them good homes!!!

While in his cage at the shelter, Cary was loving and affectionate, allowing volunteers and the staff to pet him while he rolled around and purred. I encountered Cary not long after I began volunteering for Animal Friends and decided almost immediately that I wanted to adopt him.

Once I brought him home, Cary let it be known that he didn't trust anyone when he was outside the confines and safety of his cage. Other than the note that accompanied the box containing him and his sister, I knew nothing about him or his past other than what I was able to glean from observing him at the shelter. Based on the fact that his owners abandoned him when they moved, his living situation was probably not too good.

For the first two weeks in my home, Cary hid under my bed. I fed him twice daily by sliding his food bowls under the bed and providing a dish of water he could drink from at his leisure. I placed a litter box outside the bedroom door, which he or one of the other two cats used when I was at work.

Cary, a tuxedo, and Peaches, a dilute calico, were adopted from Animal Friends by the author. (Photo courtesy of Karen Commings.)

At night when I got into bed and turned off the lights, I heard him within minutes pad down the steps to the first floor, presumably to look out of the windows at the neighborhood nightlife and socialize with the other two cats. I never heard so much as a hiss or spit from them or Cary during his nightly excursions. He apparently had no trouble accepting them. It was only his owner who had to win his trust.

One Sunday afternoon when I returned from my volunteer duties at Animal Friends just two weeks after I adopted Cary, I found him sound asleep at the foot of my bed. I entered the bedroom, changed clothes and headed back downstairs. He didn't hear me come in, nor did he run in fright. It took him two weeks to feel comfortable in the presence of his person, and since that time, Cary has become one of the most loving animals to have graced this author's surroundings. The volume of his purr has not diminished over the years, and he daily assumes a place at my side to partake of any food I am eating and any activity that occupies my time.

themselves or their kittens, ward off an intruder or win a mate. You will often observe kittens playing and seeming to bite one another gently as they roughhouse with their littermates. Your kitten or cat may become a little rough with you during play sessions, both as an outlet for her energy and as a way to continue her early kittenhood training using you as a substitute for other feline family members.

You can discourage your cat from play biting by using several techniques. First, don't play with your cat using your hands as a toy. Instead, provide her with stuffed toys that she can cling to and bite if she chooses to without hurting anyone. Cat toys are available in larger sizes for the cat that likes to wrap her legs around them and kick and bite. As a way of saving money, purchase stuffed animals of the correct size made for children. These can be found at flea markets and yard sales. Just make sure that they have no small parts that can be removed and accidentally swallowed by your cat. To attract your cat to them, sprinkle them with some catnip or open a segment of seam and insert some loose catnip before sewing it up.

Toys attached to long cords or strings can be dragged around for your cat to chase and pounce on without her pouncing on you. Interactive toys are a good way for your cat to get exercise and release that pent-up energy that has been building up all day while you were at work.

Cats need attention, love and affection. If your cat isn't getting what she needs, she may go after your ankles as you walk by to get you to notice her. Even if you are providing her with plenty of attention, she may have used this technique in her previous environment. To dissuade your cat from biting you, snap your fingers and say "No" in a firm voice when she does it. When she backs off, give her lots of praise. Reward her by spending some time engaging her in play with an interactive toy. Offer her a food treat as positive reinforcement for obeying your command. She will soon learn to let you know that she wants to play in other ways. Keep a basket full of safe toys for your cat that is easily accessible while you are at work or preoccupied. You may soon find her taking toys from the basket and bringing them to you to convince you that it's time for a play session.

Look, But Don't Touch

Cats occasionally exhibit behavior that says *look, but don't touch.* While sitting on your lap minding her own business, your cat may appear perfectly happy, but as soon as you try to pet her, her tail may begin to twitch and her hair may begin to bristle. As you continue to pet your cat, she reacts by hissing or growling, sinks her teeth into your hand and perhaps runs away. Or, your cat may rub around your legs and appear to really want you to pet her, but as soon as you do, she rewards you with a nip.

A cat may have become sensitive to being touched for any number of reasons. It may be because family members in her previous home treated her roughly; her previous owner may have teased her or rubbed her hair in the direction opposite from the way it grows (creating static buildup and discomfort). Your cat may have been tormented or pounded on by youngsters who were not taught the appropriate way to handle animals. Regardless of the reason, the experiences that caused a cat to react this way were in all probability not positive ones. Now she becomes overstimulated by the slightest touch, and the act of petting elicits a negative response that is directed at you, who only wants to give her pleasure.

As your cat's caregiver, you will need to make sure your cat has a positive home environment that does not duplicate in any way possible past negative experiences. You first will want to make sure that she feels absolutely comfortable with you and anyone else living in the household. Allow her to approach you on her own terms. Don't force her to be petted. If she is comfortable on your lap, allow her to lie there without touching her. Talk to her as usual, but don't try to pet her.

As your cat begins to adjust to you and your home, pet her in small, limited strokes behind the ears or under the chin—two places where a cat really likes to be touched. You will know if she appreciates the gesture by how she responds. If she purrs and rubs her face against your hands, the petting is pleasing to her. If she signals you to stop by twitching her tail, don't continue. Once you feel she is comfortable with being stroked in those places, begin to pet her body, again in small amounts and for a limited amount of time. If your cat purrs, you can be sure she enjoys it. Gradually, increase the amount of petting according to what she can tolerate. The important thing is to go slowly and not force her to put up with something that she finds irritating.

In extreme cases, you may want to investigate a drug therapy or a homeopathic remedy that may alter your cat's negative feelings about being touched. Discuss the options with your veterinarian.

PROFILE:
ALTERING BEHAVIOR AT TREE HOUSE

Monster Paws was a polydactyl cat who had extra toes on all four feet. He was adopted when he was six months old by a woman who moved from apartment to apartment, changing roommates virtually every month during the time she had him. As Monster Paws changed homes, he felt less and less secure both in his physical environment and in his perceived family unit. As a result, his naturally aggressive tendencies grew more and more overt. At Monster Paws' last home, he attacked and bit the landlord who, as a result, made Monster Paws' owner get rid of him. So, at the age of two, Monster Paws came to Tree House Animal Foundation, where he showed his appreciation by attacking someone at the shelter.

Monster Paws was given some hormone treatment by the Tree House medical staff and was put into a large doggy-sized crate, where he stayed in the shelter's socialization room to chill out. When the staff and volunteers were in the room, Monster Paws came out and sat on peoples' laps, but he was still uncomfortable. When the activity became too much for him, he stood by his crate and pawed the door to be let back into it.

"He had so much instability in his life," says Sandy Newbury, Tree House feline socialization specialist, "that he needed a place that was his own to make him calmer."

Taz, named after the Tasmanian Devil because of his aggressive tendencies, is one of the many cats helped by the Tree House socialization program. (Photo courtesy of Tree House Animal Foundation.)

Over time, Monster Paws became comfortable with people in the socialization room, knowing that whenever he felt the urge, he could retreat to the security of his crate. Monster Paws was adopted by a member of the Tree House staff, who took him home in the giant crate. At his new home, Monster Paws learned to trust the stability of his owner and environment. Now, the only time he wants to go in the crate is if his person has visitors he doesn't know.

"It just goes to show what you can do if you go the extra mile," says Newbury. "There is so much that can be done."

Monster Paws is just one of the cats that have been helped to overcome aggression through the Tree House socialization program. Dan had an injured foot as a stray. He was aggressive and difficult to handle when his injured foot had to be seen by a veterinarian. Once trapped, Dan came to Tree House and entered the socialization program, where he learned to trust people. He became friendly enough to be adopted into a good home.

Taz mellowed over time to give gentle sniffs instead of hostile swipes. (Photo courtesy of Tree House Animal Foundation.)

Suggs was a one-year-old cat who could be very loving but would bite when he became overstimulated. As an outlet for his energy, he engaged in play biting, which at times took on the qualities of the more aggressive cat personality. He was unpredictable and, although most of the time he was very affectionate, he could sink his teeth into someone in a split second without warning. Suggs underwent two years of therapy in the Tree House socialization program, which included play therapy with interactive toys and training him not to bite. Finally, he was adopted by a couple who didn't mind being nipped once in awhile.

At any one time, there are about 100 cats being helped to make them more adoptable by solving particular behavior problems. Shyness or aggression are two of the most common. Often, a behavior problem is precipitated by stress and uncertainty in the cat's environment, and the first step in solving it is to establish a care routine for the cat. Cats prefer stability and consistency to living in an environment that is always changing. The second step is helping the cat to once again trust humans. Treatment can take several months or even years.

The Tree House socialization program is a formal place to bring cats, step by step, to a point where they are capable of interacting with other cats and other species, including humans. Tree House has two full-time staff members devoted to the program—one socialization specialist and a caretaker who cleans the area and watches for illness in any of the cats—and many volunteers, all of whom must understand the cat's natural territorial and predatory instincts. Cats requiring medical care in addition to their behavior modification are treated by the Tree House veterinary staff.

SCRATCH AND SNIFF

Cats scratch as a form of scent marking and as a practical way of removing the sheaths from their claws. If your cat lived outside, she would be heading for the nearest tree. Inside, she is heading for a reasonable (in her mind) substitute. It is important, assuming you that want to keep your furniture intact, to provide your cat with something that will be just as attractive as a tree trunk that she can scratch instead of your expensive couch. A cat will gravitate to a scratch post, but when you bring the post home, show it to your cat and say her name so she knows that the post belongs to her. Applying a little loose catnip may help your cat want to use the post. Types of posts were described in Chapter 5, "Bringing Home Baby."

You should also let your cat know not to attack your furniture by snapping your fingers and saying "No" in a firm voice when you see her begin to claw the furniture. Some cats will stop clawing when their owners are home and save the activity for times when mom and dad are away, so providing a post is the best insurance against having your furniture cathandled when you aren't there.

Here are some additional ways you can keep Kitty from sinking her claws into your upholstered furniture:

- Cover the corners and arms of your furniture with aluminum foil or Lucite sofa ends designed specifically to deter your cat from scratching furniture. Lucite corners are advertised regularly in the Classifieds sections of the major cat magazines (see Chapter 10, "Resources").

- Purchase furniture made of fabrics that cats don't like to claw, such as velour or satin. Heavy, woven fabrics look like scratch heaven to your cat.

- Purchase furniture made of wood, such as futons, or rattan.

- Make certain rooms, such as formal living rooms, that contain your best furniture off limits to your cat.

- Spray the corners of upholstered furniture with a cat repellent, lemon juice or scent that is unappealing to cats, such as eucalyptus or cinnamon. Pretest a piece of fabric to make sure that the material can withstand the repellent.

- Experiment with different types of scratch-post surfaces. Some cats prefer sisal rope to carpet. Or, purchase a post with a variety of surfaces, including specially treated tree branches, if you're not sure what Kitty likes best.

- Place scratch posts at several places around the house.

JUMPING ON SURFACES

You may feel that certain surfaces in your house should be off limits to your cat. Many owners would prefer to keep their cats off the dining room table and kitchen counters. People are often offended by the thought of an animal stepping on a surface where food is prepared.

One of the dangers people often point to is the threat of toxoplasmosis that can be transmitted from a cat to a human. *Toxoplasmosis* is an infectious disease caused by a microscopic parasite, *Toxoplasma gondii*, commonly found in meat, mice and the feces of cats. Health experts estimate that more than 52 percent of the U.S. population has been exposed to toxoplasmosis, which in most cases causes no harm to a person. Most contact with the disease comes from eating undercooked or raw meat that contains the dormant adult organism or, because cats carry the eggs of the parasite, from gardening in places where cats have defecated.

The major threat of toxoplasmosis is to the fetus of a pregnant woman, who can develop *intrauterine growth retardation* (IUGR) if she has encountered the egg of the parasite when she cleaned the litter box of an infected cat. Because the egg is not infectious until it has been in the presence of oxygen for one to three days, it makes sense to clean the litter box as soon as a cat has defecated in it.

Many cats have been surrendered to shelters by pregnant owners who fear getting toxoplasmosis from their cats. Often pregnant women panic and dispose of their cats, assuming that simple contact with an infected animal can cause transmission of the disease. However, the likelihood of contracting this disease is just as great while you are preparing meat for dinner as it is from handling an infected cats' solid wastes. And not all cats carry toxoplasmosis, so simply having a cat in your household is no certainty that there is a danger.

If you are pregnant or thinking of having a baby, have someone else clean the litter box until your child is born to optimize safety. Most cats, like humans who have encountered toxoplasmosis, are never ill from the disease. The time following exposure during which a cat is infectious and can transmit the disease to humans is usually in the first two to three weeks. Unless a cat has an immunosuppressive disease such as FIV, once she has been exposed to toxoplasmosis, she develops a natural immunity to the disease. Keeping your cat indoors and away from strange cats will minimize exposure.

If you want to dissuade your cat from getting onto certain surface areas, whether you are concerned about toxoplasmosis, bacteria or other parasites, you can use techniques similar to those described here. When your cat jumps onto a surface that is off-limits, use the command "Down" and snap your fingers loudly. If necessary, use a gentle pressure to push your cat off the area while saying her name and using the "Down" command again. When your cat jumps down, offer her lots of praise.

Cats typically seek out counters or tabletops because there is food on them. Obviously, by keeping these surfaces as food-free as possible, they will be less attractive to your cat. Feed your cat before you begin

Rumor, a resident of Tree House, stakes a claim to the coffee cabinet. (Photo courtesy of Tree House Animal Foundation, Inc.)

preparing a meal for yourself. If your cat isn't hungry, the food you have begun to dish out for yourself won't be so appealing. Don't leave food on the countertops or table for your cat to get at when you aren't looking. Food with small bones, such as chicken, can be dangerous to your cat if ingested. The food left there also will seem like a reward for jumping on the counter.

Feeding your cat table scraps while you are having dinner in the dining room will only encourage her to make jumping on the dining-room table one of her favorite jaunts.

Some animal experts recommend "booby-trapping" places that you want your cat to avoid with stacks of soda cans or other objects that will fall and make noise, dissuading your cat from jumping by the use of fear techniques. As was mentioned before, negative reinforcement is not the best way to train your cat. Making your cat want to please you is a far better way of training her than making her afraid to disobey. From a practical standpoint, is setting up traps a way that you want to occupy your time? How useful is it to you to have a countertop full of booby-traps that you as well as your cat could knock over? If you suspect that your cat is getting on the counters or dining table in your absence, simply wiping them down before preparing food is a lot easier than setting traps that your cat may figure out how to get around anyway.

FEARS AND PHOBIAS

Your cat may show aversions to things in addition to or other than people. Loud noises, such as thunder claps, backfiring cars or fireworks can make even the most assertive and friendly feline run for cover. Some cats may even show a fear of things that will leave you scratching your head in wonder. The sound of plastic bags as you open them to line the trash can, the noise of ripping off a piece of aluminum foil to cover a food dish or even the sound of a cabinet clicking when you close it may send a cat skittering out of the room.

Although you may not be able to cure your cat of all the fears that send her into fits of frenzy, you may be able to desensitize her to at least some of the noises, particularly sounds created inside your home, such as paper or plastic rustling. A technique that can be effective is to desensitize your cat in the presence of food. The purpose is to bring about an association of the offending noise with something positive like her favorite treats.

Begin with a sound that is distant and of short duration, such as that of plastic bags rustling, while giving your cat food. Gradually move to a longer duration. You may want to offer a high-priority treat, such as bits of chicken or tuna, in the presence of the rustle to finish the association. Work on one fear at a time for each fear-inducing stimulus.

It can be very impractical to try to desensitize your cat to noises outside of the home that you can't control, such as thunder or backfiring cars. How often do you have a tape recorder in hand at the exact moment a car backfires, an excessively loud thunderclap occurs or a jet plane flies overhead so that you could play it later to gradually desensitize your cat to the noise it makes?

For situations such as these, it may be best to simply provide your cat with a place to hide. Keeping a cozy cat bed under your bed for your cat to hide in until she feels safe may be the best way to go. Allowing her to run for cover is acceptable, but don't praise or coddle her. You'll only reinforce the fear.

If your cat seems to be a bundle of nerves and jumps at the slightest sound or exhibits other behavioral symptoms as a result of her fears, discuss treating her with Valium or another anti-anxiety drug with your veterinarian.

Adjustment Blues

Most shelter cats will be grateful at being adopted and brought into a new home. Occasionally, you may find one that experiences some stress from being placed in a new environment. Signs of stress may include depression, disinterest in food, aggression, sudden failure to use the litter box, excessive grooming or failure to groom altogether, excessive meowing, or, in the extreme, self-mutilation activities like tail biting.

If your cat appears to be stressed inside your home, increase your one-on-one time with your cat. Play some soothing music and give your cat some catnip toys. As long as your cat isn't reacting negatively to touch, pet and caress her. To relieve her anxiety, avoid any drastic changes in the home. Hold a moratorium on new people or animals visiting until your cat appears comfortable and the stress signs dissipate.

A revolutionary product that can help your cat adjust to her new environment is Feliway™. Feliway contains simulated versions of naturally occurring facial pheromones—the chemical signals used to communicate among species. Pheromones are deposited on objects when a cat rubs its face against them. The presence of pheromones has a calming effect on cats and helps them initiate eating and exploratory behavior in a new environment. Spray Feliway on surfaces at your cat's eye level to increase her comfort level in her new home. Developed by scientists in France, Feliway is manufactured in a spray and is available from veterinarians.

LEASH TRAINING

Allowing an indoor cat to go with you on walks is one of the ways you can give her access to the great outdoors that is both safe and fun, but only if your cat is on a leash. As amusing as the image is to many people, particularly dog owners, cats do manage quite well walking on a leash. The willingness to wear a harness varies among cats, however, so you may have to work at getting your cat to appreciate having one on before you let her experience the great outdoors.

To begin, fit your cat with a harness, not a collar. The harness should be snug but still enable you to insert two fingers beneath it as it fits around your cat's body. Put the harness on her and allow her to wear it in the house for short periods of time. Over the course of two weeks, increase the length of time to about an hour.

Once your cat is accustomed to the harness, attach a leash. Walk around the house with her on the leash. Use gentle tugs if necessary to encourage her. Never pull her with the leash, because it will only make her resist. Talk to her and offer food treats as you walk around the house. Hold the food treat out in front of you and wait for your cat to come to you to get it. To increase her desire for the food treats, conduct training sessions before mealtimes.

Once you determine that your cat is comfortable walking with a harness and leash, take her outside to a porch or other safe area and walk for short amounts of time. Gradually increase the distance you are away from your home and your cat's safe area. If she appears frightened, take her back inside and try the lesson another time. Proceeding slowly is the best way to help your cat enjoy going for walks.

Never leave your cat tethered on a leash outside without your supervision. Anchored down, she could fall victim to another animal coming into the area and not be able to escape an attack. Even if the animal were harmless, your cat may not know that, try to run off and strangle herself with the leash.

OBEDIENCE TRAINING

Let's face it, when it comes to obedience, people give the dog credit for being the master. *Come, Stand, Sit, Stay* and *Down* are all commands associated with dog training, and dogs that have graduated from some sort of obedience program love to show what they can do. On the training end, cats have been given a bum rap.

But turn on your television or go out to a movie, and you'll see lots of feline stars performing in precisely the ways that producers and directors want them to. These cats may not light up the silver screen as well as the dogs in *101 Dalmatians*, but cats perform commands on queue just like their canine counterparts, and they didn't learn to do so with ESP.

Yes, you can train your cat to do all sorts of tricks by using the same techniques as professional animal trainers who prepare felines for lives in the movies or on television. You may not want to train your cat to perform tricks, but training her to understand and obey a few common commands will help you strengthen your relationship with her, help her understand what you expect and may actually prevent accidents involving your cat.

Imagine that you are about to go out the door of your house or apartment. You have your arms full of packages that you are taking to the car. Your cat, naturally curious about what you are doing and eager to become involved in your activities, follows you to the door. You can barely turn the doorknob to let yourself out, much less free both hands to push your cat back to keep her from escaping. You put down the packages and push her back, telling her "No." You pick up the packages to leave again, only to have her follow you once more. Frustrated and fearful for your cat's safety should she go outside, you once again put down the packages, this time taking Kitty to a room where you close her in so she cannot get out. Now your cat is frustrated and begins to meow and dig at the carpet under the door to get out of the room. After all, none of her cat stuff is in the room to keep her occupied and amused.

Sound unlikely? Just ask your cat-owning friends how often this scenario has occurred in their homes. Then ask them how often their cats escaped by accident when someone held the door open too long. If this seems like something that just might happen at your house, wouldn't it be nice to be able to issue one command like *Sit* or *Stay* and have your cat stop in her tracks immediately and go no farther?

Many people may wonder why it is important to teach cats commands that are similar to those commonly taught dogs in obedience school. Isn't it just wonderful allowing a cat to be a cat, independently off on her own and doing what comes naturally? Do you need to have your cat obey on command? If one of your friends or acquaintances ever experiences the heartbreak of having a cat injured or perhaps killed because she escaped out an open door, they will understand that obedience training may help prevent such a tragedy from happening to your cat.

One of the most successful cat trainers is Scott Hart. Hart developed a multi-step method of training his cats that appear on television, in commercials, in public appearances and in the movies. His method uses positive reinforcement of food rewards when the cat performs the command correctly. The method is called *conditioned response*, and it works on your cat just as it did with Pavlov's dogs.

Conditioned response is already working in your household when your cat charges into the kitchen when you run the can opener or when your cat goes to the window at 5:15 p.m. waiting for your car to pull into the driveway. Using conditioned response to train your cat to obey commands is just a continuation of what has been occurring naturally as you both go about your daily routines. When you train your cat, you will be reinforcing a specific behavior with a specific food reward and a sound that your cat will associate with the reward.

The use of a sudden sound to distract your cat from doing something she should not do was discussed earlier in this chapter. A clap or snap of the fingers will cause your cat to pause and redirect her energy. Saying "No" in a firm voice will enable her to associate the command with the sound. When training your cat to obey commands, you will be using another sound—that of a clicker—to enable your cat to associate the sound in a positive way with receiving the food reward. Clickers are frequently used in dog training and can be purchased at pet supply stores.

To train your cat, do it before she has eaten her regular meal to maximize her interest in food as a reward. Don't starve your cat in order to train her. Train your cat in a location that is free of distractions or noises. Give the process your complete attention and don't allow it to compete with other stimuli such as television. As a food reward, select something your cat really likes but does not get very often, such as bits of chicken or baby food. Keep the training session to about ten to fifteen minutes at a time, so that your cat does not become tired. Be consistent with the words you use for the command. It will only confuse your cat if you say "Come" on some occasions and "Here" on others.

To associate the food with a sound, obtain a clicker or child's small cricket. When you feed your cat her regular meals, make the clicking sound so she begins to associate the sound with eating. After you have done this for a week or so, go to your cat's regular feeding station and make the clicking sound. If she comes, she has associated the sound with being fed, and you can now begin the specific training. Be sure to offer her food on this occasion so she continues to make the connection.

During training sessions, always use your cat's name along with the command you are trying to teach. In addition to the food reward, pet and praise your cat when she performs the behavior you desire. Always use the clicker at the moment your cat is performing the behavior you want.

In all of the command training, Hart recommends that you have a table for the cat to sit or lie down on. It is also possible to conduct the training on the floor, but you will have to bend over each time you offer the food reward or hold it over your cat's head to get her attention. To train your cat, have all necessary materials at hand. Before trying to teach a command, decide what word you will use for each command you want to teach, and use it consistently. Teach only one command at a time and for short periods of time at each lesson. Repeat the lesson daily until your cat has learned the command. Once she has learned the command, move on to the next one.

Sit or Stay

What a wonderful device for ensuring that the scenario of your cat escaping outdoors never happens. To teach your cat to sit or stay, decide first what word you will use. Hart recommends placing your cat on the corner of a table and holding the food reward over her head. Say your cat's name and give the command "Sit." As her head follows the food, she will naturally sit down. Make the clicking sound and say "Sit." If your cat sits to follow the food, give her the food reward immediately. You might have to encourage her to sit by pressing lightly on her hindquarters. As you do, continue to hold the food over her head and say "Sit." When she sits, make the clicking sound and give her the food right away. Soon, your cat will begin to associate the food reward with the command, and you will no longer have to use the clicker to make her sit. Simply saying "Sit" will be enough.

Continue the pattern until your cat begins to associate the command and the clicking noise with the food. If your cat appears to be frustrated or impatient, save the lesson for another time.

Come

You may think that it's demeaning for a cat to come on command, but until you try to get your cat into a cat carrier when it's time to visit the veterinarian and have her hide under the bed as soon as you take the carrier out of the closet, you'll never know how useful such a command can be. And isn't it better to have her associate coming to you with something positive instead of something negative at a moment like that?

Once your cat comes to her feeding station at the sound of the clicker, begin training her to come at the sound of the command "Come." Hart recommends saying your cat's name, giving the command "Come" and then pressing the clicker a few times. When your cat comes, press the clicker again and praise her. Give her the food reward immediately.

Continue this process, but from new locations around your house. Your cat should eventually come to you at the sound of the command alone without the need for you to use the clicker. Remember to praise her and offer her a food reward for obeying the command.

You can use these same techniques to get your cat to learn other commands like "Down" so that making her jump down off a surface you don't want her on becomes a pleasant experience for both of you.

CAT SHRINKS

Okay. So you've tried everything, and you just can't get your cat to behave in the ways you want. You've given up trying to impart a lesson on what seems like an untrainable cat. What do you do when your cat is driving you crazy? Call on the services of a cat shrink—a person who helps you modify your cat's behavior so that it is more satisfying to you. Yes, to help *you* modify your cat's behavior. Don't expect anyone, regardless of credentials, training or experience, to come to your home and wave a magic wand and get Kitty to start using her litter box immediately or to make her never want to claw your sofa again. The solution to any behavior problem will mean that you, as well as your cat, will have to participate. It may mean modifying your behavior or changing your lifestyle to accommodate the needs of your cat. So, be prepared to follow the advice of your cat's psychiatrist.

No government agency regulates animal behavior, and no state license is required to practice animal behavior consulting as is required to practice veterinary medicine. Anyone can put up a sign that says *Kitty Shrink* and call himself an animal behaviorist. If you are frustrated with your cat's behavior, first discuss it with your veterinarian. Veterinarians are trained to offer some behavioral assistance with animals, so your veterinarian is a good place to start.

Many of the larger shelters offer behavior assistance to pet owners as part of their other services. Both the San Francisco SPCA and the Denver Dumb Friends League, for example, operate behavior hot lines that anyone can call. Of course, you may have to call long distance, but the call will certainly be less expensive than replacing your sofa or your stereo speakers if your cat is in the process of ripping them to shreds. Ask if the shelter from which you adopted your cat has such a service available or if the staff can recommend one.

In addition to behavior hot lines operated by shelters, there are behavior lines run by professional services. Such services are operated as 900 numbers, and you pay for the call or for listening to a tape on a particular topic, such as aggression or litter-box problems. The Internet and World Wide Web, as well as printed resources, offer other avenues for solving your cat's behavior problem.

If you would like to obtain the services of a professional applied animal behavior consultant, contact the Animal Behavior Society (see Chapter 10, "Resources"). The Animal Behavior Society is the professional organization for those who have obtained a master's degree or doctorate in animal behavior. The organization certifies individuals to become animal behavior consultants by requiring that they pass a written test and provide at least two letters of recommendation from other professionals in the field. Certified animal behavior consulting is a relatively new field, and there are only a few dozen such specialists across the country. Most applied animal behaviorists will want to observe your cat in her home environment, which limits you to finding one near you. If none are available in your region, you may be forced to seek other means to solve your cat's behavior problem or to pay a consultant to travel to you.

CHAPTER 8

If You Really Want a Breed

Well, maybe what you really want is not a domestic shorthaired shelter cat after all, but a purebred that has a long bloodline of champions in his background. Perhaps you simply fell in love when you saw a magazine photo of an endearing Scottish Fold kitten with his ears lying tightly against his head. Maybe one of your friends has an impish Abyssinian that delights you with his antics every time you pay a visit. Or, perhaps you think a cobby, tailless Manx might be a cat with which you and your children could bond.

If you are visiting shelters in the hope that one of these purebred cats will show up some day and be there for you to adopt him, forget it. The Humane Society of the United States estimates that 25 percent of all dogs entering shelters are purebreds. These animals could be from breeding programs and sold as pets to owners who disposed of them. Many of these animals are from people considered to be backyard breeders who, once they obtain a dog that is registered with the American Kennel Club, decide to let it have a litter of puppies. They give the puppies to friends who don't keep them, or they sell them to make a few dollars. The new owners, because they have little or no monetary investment in the animal, feel free to discard the dog when it becomes inconvenient.

With purebred cats, it's a different story. For some unknown reason, owners of purebred cats do not give them up to shelters readily. It is extremely unlikely that you will find cats in most of the breeds in your local shelter. Occasionally, you'll find a Persian that had an owner who didn't keep up with the grooming necessary to keep the Persian coat smooth and tangle-free. Maybe you'll find a Siamese whose loud talking annoyed his owner. Once in a while, you might find a cat that resembles a British Shorthair or one that has no tail, which incidentally, does not make a cat a Manx. But if you really want to adopt a cat of a specific breed, your best bet is to go elsewhere.

CAT SHOWS

If you think that you're interested in adopting a particular breed of cat, the best place to start is to visit a cat show. Cat shows are run by cat clubs affiliated with national cat registries. Unlike dog clubs, most of which are affiliated with the American Kennel Club, cat shows can be hosted by clubs belonging to any one of six national cat registries: the Cat Fanciers' Association (CFA), The International Cat Association (TICA), the American Cat Association (ACA), the American Cat Fanciers' Association (AFCA), the Cat Fanciers' Federation (CFF) and the United Cat Federation (UCF). The Cat Fanciers' Association is the largest breed association in the world.

Cat shows occur throughout most of the year all over the United States. Finding one in your area is as simple as checking the listings in one of the national cat magazines, such as *Cat Fancy*, *CATS* or *I Love Cats* or contacting a cat club in your area. Typically, these magazines list shows chronologically one or two months in advance.

Once at the show, you will be able to browse the exhibits and see many beautiful purebred cats. There are more than thirty breeds, but not all cat registries recognize each of them. You can talk to specific breeders about what the breed is like and what makes a cat a champion, if you think that showing cats may be in your future. You may even find some kittens for sale at the show. But beware: The price of show-quality, purebred kittens can be pretty steep, so plan on spending some money.

Even if you're only looking and have no intention of buying, cat shows are a great place to learn about the different breeds. They also are wonderful places to find products for you and your cat, whether he is a purebred or not. You'll find lots of products that you may never see in retail stores and some offered at lower prices than you'll find in your local pet stores. Cat beds, grooming supplies, cat treats and samples from pet-food manufacturers, interactive and catnip cat toys and cat climbing trees are just some of the items you'll find on display at cat shows.

If you've adopted a domestic shorthaired cat from a shelter, he may still be able to be exhibited at a cat show and compete in the Happy Household Pet Cat (HHPC) category. The HHPC is the category in which cats that are not purebreds or are pet-quality breeds compete for ribbons just like their purebred counterparts. Even if you don't have a purebred cat, you may want to enjoy the fun and excitement of competition that occurs at cat shows by showing your cat.

Cats that are shown in the HHPC must be altered if they are more than eight months of age. They must be healthy and carry no contagious diseases, have clean coats and clear eyes, be well-behaved and be easy to handle. If you think that you'd like to show your pet cat, contact a regional cat club or a club sponsoring an upcoming show for rules, regulations and procedures.

BREEDERS

The breed profiles and breeder listings found in cat magazines are a good way to get information pertaining to purebred cats. Each month, the cat magazines highlight a specific breed. The articles frequently are written by a breeder who is knowledgeable about the breed, its temperament, personality and the standards to which it should conform to make it show quality. Reading up on each breed may help you decide if a particular one is right for you.

After you've settled on one or two breeds that you would like to investigate, look in the breeder directories in the magazines. Not every area of the country will have catteries representative of each breed, but you will be able to locate the cattery closest to you. Breeder directories are usually listed toward the back of each major cat magazine.

The Cat Fanciers' Association offers breeder-referral listings for anyone wanting to find a specific breed in a particular area of the country. For example, you may want a listing of Siamese breeders in New Jersey. If you send CFA a stamped, self-addressed envelope with the request, they will send you the names of the breeders, their cities and states, telephone numbers and descriptions of colors. See Chapter 10, "Resources," for the address of the Cat Fanciers' Association.

If you're hooked up to the Internet and World Wide Web, the Cat Fanciers' Association has a beautiful and informative home page. On it, you'll find information and photographs of the thirty-three breeds recognized by the CFA. You'll also find a listing of upcoming cat shows, cat-care information, legislative issues and background information of the CFA. (See Chapter 10, "Resources," for the CFA Web address.)

The Pet Channel's Animal Network, a service of Fancy Publications, publishers of *Cat Fancy* magazine, offers a guide to finding breeds on its Web site. Click on the breed that appeals to you and find a description and photo of the breed and listings of breeders in the state of your choice. See Chapter 10, "Resources," for the Web address of the Animal Network's Feline Finder.

If finances are a concern to you, talk to a breeder about purchasing a pet-quality kitten rather than one that conforms to all the standards of the show ring. Often, breeders have some kittens that, for one reason or another, do not make good show cats and therefore will not become part of the show circuit or any breeding program. Breeders may offer these kittens to a good home at a lower price than show-quality kittens.

In addition to kittens, breeders have older cats they may be looking to place into good homes. The older cats may be retired from the show ring, or the cattery may be looking to reduce the number of cats it houses. A female may be too old to produce litters of kittens. Typically, such a cat will be mellow, spayed or neutered, have no contagious or life-threatening diseases and be current on all vaccinations.

A prospective pet parent can find lovely cats that simply may be too old to compete. These cats will make wonderful pets for someone willing to offer them a loving home. They have set personalities, and the cattery owner will be familiar with their dispositions and temperaments. Adopting one of these older cats may be more affordable than adopting a purebred kitten or show cat.

CHAPTER 9

In
Service
to
Others

As much as shelters cry out for responsible people to adopt their animals, they also have a need for people who want to donate their time and talents to helping shelters conduct their business. Everyone who loves animals, regardless of whether they feel they have a talent, has something to offer a shelter and its animals, even if it's only for two or three hours a week cleaning cages or talking to and playing with the cats and dogs living there.

If you are thinking about volunteering your time for a shelter, you may want to first examine your feelings about euthanasia. For someone who has difficulty accepting euthanasia, volunteering at a shelter that must put to death the animals that are not adopted can be emotionally taxing. So, instead of having a positive, rewarding experience, you may be faced week after week with an emotionally trying one. Before offering your time to a shelter, ask yourself how you will cope with knowing that more than half of the animals you pet, groom and play with may die before you see them again. If you feel you can manage it, then volunteering for a shelter that euthanizes should not be an issue for you.

VOLUNTEERS APLENTY

A recent issue of *Pet Tales*, the newsletter of the Denver Dumb Friends League, itemized the efforts of its volunteer staff. Volunteers work in areas such as adoptions, offer animal behavior assistance, serve on the board of directors, and perform community service by assisting in the kennels and grooming. They also work in the Pet Lost and Found department, conduct community outreach (such as humane education and pet visitation) and offer assistance in their Veterinary Services department. The volunteers of the Denver Dumb Friends League logged more than 54,000 hours of work in a year. That was the equivalent of twenty-seven full-time employees. When you add up the costs for staffing with paid employees, it becomes apparent just how important volunteers are to a shelter. It's safe to say that none could operate as effectively without the services of pet lovers just like you.

If you feel that you have some time to spend or talent to donate, shelters offer a whole range of activities in which you could participate. Most will try to find volunteer work that suits your skills. As a person who volunteers, you should have certain expectations from the shelter staff members. First, they should train you adequately to perform the task for which you are volunteering. They also should alert you to the rules and regulations of the shelter and provide you with information about how it operates. And they should introduce you to full-time staff members who will let you know what is expected. It does a shelter no good to have volunteers on hand who want to work but have no idea what to do because the staff is too busy to guide them.

A shelter also should be able to expect certain things from you as a volunteer. If you would like to volunteer at a shelter, make sure that you have the time to give. Once you've offered your time and have committed to doing a particular job at a particular time, be dependable. If you've committed to working in a shelter-run retail store on a Saturday, take that commitment seriously. The shelter, its staff and other volunteers are depending on you. As pointless as it is for you to volunteer at a shelter that has not taken the time to educate you regarding the tasks it desires you to perform, it is also pointless for you to offer to do a particular job and not show up when you are supposed to. The work still must get done, and shelter staff members or other volunteers will have to do it in your absence. Not knowing what to expect from you may delay them in finding someone on whom they can rely. If you feel as if your heart is bigger than your head when it comes to volunteer work, wait until you have time instead of forcing yourself into an untenable position.

If you are interested in volunteering, shelters have a wealth of volunteer job opportunities from which you can select. Talk to the staff at the shelter that interests you or from which you adopted your cat to see what volunteer duties it may have available.

PET THERAPY

Many shelters offer pet-therapy programs where staff and volunteers take animals with specific temperaments to local nursing homes, hospitals, treatment centers or even schools. Pets offer companionship and unconditional love to the residents of these facilities, many of whom had pets in their younger days or when they could care for them. By stroking a cat or petting a dog, residents find solace and comfort. Unresponsive patients often come out of their shells when allowed to interact with an animal. At schools, pets and volunteers help teach children a love and respect for other living creatures.

Both dogs and cats can be used as therapy volunteers along with their human companions, although the practice more often employs the services of a Fido than a Fluffy. Typically, animals must be willing to be petted and handled by strangers. Therapy pets must be healthy and free of fleas and other parasites. They should be well-trained and enjoy socializing. Needless to say, the proverbial nipper should not be allowed to accompany its human companion to a nursing home to inflict pain on unsuspecting residents who want to partake of the joys of pet ownership.

Shelters that operate a pet-assisted therapy program usually have resident animals that they use but may be looking for human volunteers who will fit the bill. If you would like to be involved in this emotionally rewarding activity, contact your local shelter. If no therapy program is available, contact the Delta Society for information about its Pet Partners program.

Lynette Hart, a blind volunteer, socializes cats at Animal Friends, Inc. (Photo courtesy of Margaret G. Stanley, Animal Friends, Inc.)

SOCIALIZING

You have read about the importance of socializing animals and what it may mean to you as a new pet owner. Shelters use volunteers in different ways to socialize their animals, but in all cases it involves working hands on with the animals. At some shelters, socializing may simply mean taking the animals out of their cages and petting and playing with them to help alleviate the stress of confinement. At other shelters, socializing may be part of an overall behavior-modification program.

If you'd like to opportunity to help Buster learn not to bite, to help Sheila become less shy or to simply make their days a little more pleasant until a special person comes along to offer them a good, permanent home, socializing cats may be a volunteer job that seems more like play than work.

GETTING THE WORD OUT

Shelters use a variety of techniques to get their message to the pet-owning public and would-be pet owners. They issue newsletters, special flyers and press releases about upcoming events. If you have a knack for writing, offering your talents in preparing these messages may be a great way for you to volunteer. It also may give you the opportunity to work out of your home if getting to the shelter on a regular basis is difficult for you.

If you have a home computer, you can help a shelter by performing newsletter layout and design, writing articles or preparing press releases that describe upcoming events for local newspapers. If you know about printing techniques, you can work with local printers to give the materials a professional look.

Shelters often need someone who can record special events or take photos of the shelter animals, staff and volunteers for shelter newsletters. Think about assisting in taking photographs if you are good with a camera.

CYBER ASSISTANCE

Is working with computers your bag? Do you like to sit in front of a computer screen for hours on end? Do you have a flair for graphic design? If you answered yes to these questions, you may want to offer your skills as a Webmaster designing a Web home page for your local shelter.

If you look at the list in of shelters in Chapter 10, "Resources", you'll discover that virtually all of them have their own home pages. Designing and setting up a home page requires a knowledge of hypertext markup language (HTML) as well as good graphic-design principles. Very few shelters can afford to hire someone to design a Web page for them. If you have these skills and access to some disk storage space through your local Internet service provider, you may want to offer to set up a home page for a shelter near you.

PROFILE:
HELPING HANDS AT THE PASADENA HUMANE SOCIETY

Assisting the forty-four full-time staff members at the Pasadena Humane Society are more than 350 volunteers who perform a plethora of functions. Many of them socialize the animals by petting, brushing and playing with them. Others who want the experience become veterinary assistants.

The shelter also uses adoption counselors and assistants, outreach specialists, pet-therapy volunteers, foster pet parents, office assistants and health-staff assistants.

"Most people want hands-on experience with the animals," says Sandy DeMarco, Pasadena's full-time volunteer coordinator who helps match volunteers with appropriate tasks as well as oversees the volunteer operation. "Maybe they live in an apartment that doesn't allow pets. Here, they can branch out. We encourage them to work."

Volunteers begin with a three-hour orientation on a Saturday morning. They see a slide show about the Pasadena Humane Society and learn about its operation. Volunteers meet the head of each department and hear about what they do. Every volunteer must undergo kennel training, which includes how to access the animals and the regulations for being an on-site volunteer. If people want to do a specific job, they go to the department and talk to the folks who work there.

DeMarco began her job in the early 1990s when the shelter had only twenty-six volunteers but lots of work to do. "It was sort of a create-a-job," she jokes. "Now I have more volunteers than I know what to do with. People love working with animals."

INSIDE THE KENNEL

Many shelters have full-time staff members who regularly feed the animals and clean their cages, but some do not. Helping to keep the shelter running and taking care of the animals' necessities is a task that many shelters rely on their volunteers to perform. Some shelters, such as the Helen Opperman Krause Animal Foundation, are run entirely by volunteers, so offering to do just the basics is warmly welcomed.

Kennel work can include cleaning the litter pans and food dishes, refilling them, cleaning out the cages or the kennel floors and making the area appealing to the animals and the visitors who come to adopt them. A clean kennel is one of the most telling signs about a shelter and how it operates, so it is very important to help the shelter perform this function.

SOLICITATIONS

Is talking to people and asking for their help something that really turns you on? Does getting out into the community and disseminating the word about the important work the shelter does appeal to you? If this kind of work is what you were destined for, shelters can always use people to conduct solicitations for them.

Not all the solicitations are for money. If the shelter is holding an auction, for example, it will need people to solicit local businesses to contribute new items for the auction. Assisting in this activity (and providing the organization with a receipt for income-tax purposes at the time of the donation) is another way to help.

Some solicitations involve standing on street corners with a well-behaved shelter pet and asking passersby to put donations in a can. Other solicitations involve going from door to door asking for contributions or asking people to purchase items the shelter is selling to raise money, such as candy. Some are for items to donate to a shelter-run garage or yard sale. Perhaps the shelter needs local businesses to agree to house a money canister in which shoppers can deposit their change at the cash registers. If you're willing to pound the pavement, ask your shelter what volunteer opportunities are available for you.

Volunteers staff a booth to sell items for an animal organization as part of a shopping mall pet fair. (Photo courtesy of Karen Commings.)

ADOPTION COUNSELORS

Remember when you went to a shelter and inquired about a particular cat and someone helped you select the one that suited your personality and lifestyle? Chances are that that person was a volunteer working as an adoption counselor.

Adoption counselors receive special training and learn how to ask the right questions of prospective pet parents to determine what kind of animal they want to adopt. They pay special attention to the animals at the shelter to learn about their temperaments and personalities and to match them with the right people. If interacting directly with people and animals appeals to you, adoption counseling might be right up your alley.

PROFILE:
LEARNING TO HELP AT THE
HUMANE SOCIETY OF HARRISBURG AREA

In 1997, the Humane Society of Harrisburg Area (HSHA) was faced with limited staffing and began a formal program of training volunteers to help people who want to adopt a pet. The goal of the program was to increase the number of people who could serve as adoption counselors and match the right pet with the right person. Ultimately, the society would like to have an adoption counselor volunteer on duty every hour the shelter is open.

At the orientation program, prospective adoption counselors learn about the shelter, its policies and procedures, what questions are most frequently asked and how to provide the appropriate answers. They are given hands-on training on how to help someone correctly take a pet out of its cage and to make sure that the animal is put back in the right one.

"This gives them an opportunity to see what it's really like," says Linda Spangler, HSHA Development Coordinator. As more volunteers come on board, they are paired with a trained volunteer until the next seminar is held.

The Humane Society of Harrisburg Area operates two shelters in the greater Harrisburg, Pennsylvania, area. In 1997, the society began a major building campaign to expand its facilities.

Foster Parenting

Occasionally, shelters obtain animals, especially kittens or puppies, that need an extra bit of attention to make them adoptable. Perhaps the kittens lost their mother and need to be bottle fed. Or, perhaps the cat or dog has a health problem that needs to be treated before it can be put into the kennel or go into a home. Such animals are first given to temporary foster homes, where they are given that extra amount of TLC to make them ready for adoption into permanent homes.

Good foster programs have a set of guidelines for the foster parents to follow. For example, foster homes are not to be used simply as additional cage space when the shelter becomes overcrowded. They should be for animals who have a good chance of finding a home once some preliminary health or behavior problems are resolved. Foster programs should not become secondary adoption agencies, and all animals being fostered should go back to the shelter for adoption through its regular placement department. Foster pets should not be allowed contact with the pets living in the foster parent's household to prevent the potential spread of diseases.

Two cats share the attention of a volunteer in the Tree House Animal Foundation's Foster Parent office. (Photo courtesy of Tree House Animal Foundation, Inc.)

Foster parenting can be both emotionally rewarding and emotionally trying. No matter how objective a foster parent is, letting the fostered animals go can be tough. Fostering is a job that can be done at home. If you have some extra space in your home and your heart to temporarily take in a needy cat or kitten until it recovers from an illness or becomes old enough to be adopted into a permanent home, fostering may be the volunteer activity for you.

GROOMING

Do you have a knack for bathing a cat or painlessly removing knots from its hair? An animal that is well groomed will reflect it in its personality. An animal that looks good also feels good. Some shelters operate in-house grooming facilities that help their animals feel better about themselves and make the pet more appealing to prospective pet parents.

Even if you've never groomed animals before, staff members at a shelter operating a grooming facility will be able to train you to help out. Most animals that are groomed are dogs, but cats need to be groomed on occasion, too. Not all shelters that need groomers may have an in-house facility. Often, the grooming effort is centered around periodic dog washes. Regardless, if you're not afraid to get your hands wet or have the necessary grooming skills, ask your shelter if it needs someone who wants to groom animals.

VETERINARY SERVICES

Shelters have a need for people who can assist veterinarians with helping sick or injured animals. Such volunteers have a variety of titles, such as veterinary technicians, veterinary assistants, health-care aids, surgery assistants and animal handlers. Some shelters require specialized education, but others offer on-the-job training for anyone interested. Some young volunteers use such work as a way to obtain experience prior to entering veterinary school or to work toward a veterinary technician degree.

Veterinary assistant volunteers give shots and medication, bring animals from their cages to surgery or exam rooms and assist the shelter's veterinary staff in a variety of other ways. If you'd like to contribute your time assisting in the health care of shelter animals, you may enjoy veterinary assistance work.

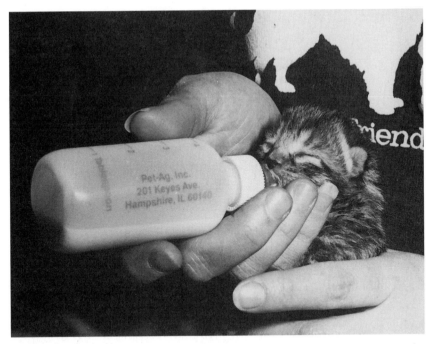

A volunteer veterinary assistant at Animal Friends, Inc., bottle-feeds a kitten too young to be adopted. (Photo courtesy of Margaret G. Stanley, Animal Friends, Inc.)

OFFICE ASSISTANT

Filling out forms, keeping track of adoptions and incoming animals, assisting adopters with their applications, answering phones, doing mailings, renewing pet licenses and keeping computer records are just some of the tasks performed by volunteer office assistants. While office duties may seem like bureaucratic red tape to some, these functions are important to shelters that must keep records of their animals even once they've left the shelter. If you are highly organized and can contribute some time to a shelter, helping it keep ahead of its paperwork might be a way to spend your volunteer time.

LOST AND FOUND

Shelters are the first places people look when they've lost a beloved pet. Nothing is more heartwarming than being able to reunite a lost pet with its frantic owner. Many shelters ask volunteers to help pet owners locate lost pets through kennel inspections and newspaper ads. Working in the

Lost and Found department will mean using office or communications skills by answering the shelter telephone.

PET PLACEMENT FOLLOWUP

Shortly after you adopted your shelter cat, someone called you from the shelter to ask how things were going. It is likely that that person was a volunteer who donated his or her time to placing phone calls to recent adopters to follow up on the pet's condition and ask how the animal was doing in her new home.

Volunteers who do pet placement followup should be friendly, courteous and have a sincere interest in the person and the pet. They should know that the shelter wants the situation to work out and be willing to offer whatever shelter resources are available to ensure that it does. The individual should be able to provide basic care advice and should know how to access information for the new pet owner. A pet-placement followup volunteer should have a pleasing telephone voice and manner and be willing to communicate with the adopter.

Being a pet-placement volunteer is one more good idea for people who like dealing with other people who like pets.

PROFILE:
RECOGNIZING THE IMPORTANCE OF VOLUNTEERS

Like other shelters, Animal Friends, Inc., knows how important its volunteer staff is to the operation of its shelter and the care of the animals in it. To help volunteers learn about the shelter and the work they must do, Animal Friends has prepared a volunteer manual that contains guidelines for working at the shelter. It has photos of the full-time staff and their names and titles. The manual addresses volunteer procedures upon arrival, how to care for the cats and dogs and how to handle them properly. It also includes a history of the shelter and a checklist for volunteers who walk dogs and care for cats.

Animal Friends asks its volunteers to keep track of the hours they spend doing tasks such as walking, exercising and grooming dogs and cats, planning or helping at special events and fund raisers, helping office staff, working at rabies clinics and PetSmart vaccination clinics, going on pet-therapy visits and doing the many other activities in which volunteers become involved.

A volunteer at Animal Friends typically donates nine hours per month. When a volunteer reaches fifty hours of service, volunteers receive shelter mailings. At 100 hours of service, he or she receives an official Animal Friends name tag and is qualified to attend the shelter's volunteer recognition dinner offered at half price. When a volunteer reaches 200 hours of service, he or she receives an Animal Friends T-shirt. At 400 hours, volunteers receive a rain poncho or hat. Volunteer hours are tabulated by another volunteer who compiles the data during the first week of each month.

These are just some of the ways that a shelter can reward volunteers for their hours of service.

HOME HANDY WORK

Is baking your bag? Do you have a talent for putting together attractive craft items for sale to the public? Shelters often sponsor craft sales or bake sales that raise money for the shelter. If you like to cook or do crafts, ask your shelter if and when it is sponsoring any events that might use your talents. Like some of the other volunteer activities mentioned, baking or doing crafts can be done out of your home if you have trouble getting to the shelter once a week.

LETTER WRITER

Shelters often take an active role in their communities by sponsoring or supporting various legislative efforts that contribute to the welfare of

A volunteer offers handmade craft items for sale at a pet fair. (Photo courtesy of Karen Commings.)

animals. Or shelters may oppose legislation that they feel is harmful to animals' welfare. You can help in those efforts by lobbying your legislative representatives—local, state or federal—to support or oppose various animal-related bills that might be before them.

Shelters may ask its membership to take a stand on upcoming legislation via their newsletters. If you see a request for help in a shelter mailing, pick up paper and pen or computer and keyboard and let your legislator know how you feel.

FINANCIAL CONTRIBUTIONS

No matter how many volunteers a shelter has, it still needs money to operate. Animals need to be fed, buildings need to be maintained and animals and people need to have electricity and heat. If you would rather donate cash than time, or perhaps both, your local animal shelter will be grateful for any offer of money you are willing to make.

Many shelters offer opportunities during their fiscal years for people to contribute even small amounts. For example, your shelter may have a holiday tree for which you may purchase a $5.00 light or ornament in honor or memory of a pet. Memberships in shelters often come in several levels so you can select the level that suits your financial situation. If you are a student or a senior citizen, for example, the cost of membership may be less than that for others. A working adult may usually choose from several membership levels. Shelters also may have opportunities for contributors to donate costs associated with special projects. If a shelter is expanding its facilities, it may seek donations for the cost of a room or a single animal cage where the contributor sees a plaque placed at the room entrance or on the cage with her or his name on it.

On a larger scale, many people have been known to make a shelter a beneficiary in their wills. Regardless of the amount of the donation you may be able to give, every bit helps. So, if you have a little money to spare, make a donation to your local shelter.

PROFESSIONAL SERVICES

If you would prefer to donate your professional services instead of, or in addition to a monetary donation, many shelters would love to have you on board. Perhaps you are a computer programmer or know how to set up a personal computer database. Maybe your shelter would love to get those intake and adoption forms in good order so that they could be easily accessed.

Perhaps you have a small business, such as a remodeling company, and you can contribute in-kind services such as conducting minor building repairs. Or, perhaps you own an office-supply company that could donate filing cabinets, paper or other office supplies.

If you or your small business would like to donate goods or services to a shelter for ongoing operation or a specific project, contact it to determine how best to help.

HUMANE EDUCATION

Shelter volunteers often go to schools and community-service organizations to talk about animals and how to care for them properly. They also may conduct in-house tours and presentations for groups interested in learning about the work of the shelter.

If standing in front of an audience interests you, and you are knowledgeable about animal care and animal issues, offering your time to help conduct humane-education lessons may be a good activity for you.

SPAY/NEUTER FOLLOWUP

Shelters require that cats and dogs adopted from them are spayed or neutered. Animals too young to be altered by the shelter must be altered when they are of age by the new owners, and non-altered adult animals must also be altered. Shelters need volunteers to help follow up with the pet parent to help ensure that the important surgery has been completed. This may involve sending postcards or making telephone calls.

ANIMAL CONTROL AND CRUELTY

Shelters often have on-staff cruelty investigators and animal-control officers whose job it is to investigate allegations of animal abuse, pick up injured or dead animals and confiscate animals living in inhumane circumstances. Performing such tasks involves obtaining specialized training.

Shelters may need extra humane officers in times of emergency. If you think you may have the special skills required to do such work or are willing to obtain the skills, contact your local shelter to see if it needs humane-officer volunteers.

SHOPS

Some shelters operate facilities within the shelter that sell shelter-related items. Very often, the shelter shop is staffed by volunteers who sell merchandise to the public.

The Marin Humane Society, for example, runs a thrift shop that nets the society more than $35,000.00 a year, enabling the shelter to offer affordable spay/neuter surgery. The thrift shop is staffed by volunteers who are willing to work one day per month.

If you'd like to offer your services retailing shelter items or other items in support of your shelter, ask what it may have available for you to do.

CHAPTER 10

Resources

ASSOCIATIONS

American Holistic Veterinary Medical Association

For a list of holistic veterinarians in your area, send a stamped, self-addressed envelope to

> American Holistic Veterinary
> Medical Association
> 2214 Old Emmorton road
> Bel Air, MD 21014

Or, visit its Web site at

> http://www.altvetmed.com/
> associat.html

It includes an online membership directory by state and treatment method, such as homeopathy, acupuncture or herbal medicine.

Animal Behavior Society

For a list of certified animal behaviorists, send a stamped, self-addressed envelope to

> Animal Behavior Society
> Dr. John C. Wright
> Certified Animal Behaviorist
> Department of Psychology
> Mercer University
> Macon, GA 31207

Or contact Dr. Wright via electronic mail at

wright_jc@mercer.edu

Visit the Animal Behavior Society Web site at

http://www.cisab.indiana.edu/animal_behaviour.html

Breed Rescue
Contact the Abyssinian and Somali rescue in writing, or visit their Web site at

S.A.B.R.E.
P.O. Box 838
Cary, IL 60013
http://www.tezcat.com/~ermiller/somrescue.html

Cat Fanciers' Association
For a list of breeders in your area, write to them at

Cat Fanciers' Association
P.O. Box 1005
Manasquan, NJ 08736-0805

Or visit its Web site at

http://www.cfainc.org/

Happy Household Pet Cat Club
For membership information, send a stamped, self-addressed envelope to

Florine Jones
8862 Sharkey Avenue
Elk Grove, CA 95624

Or, visit its Web site at

http://shell5.ba.best.com:80/~slewis/HHPCC/

Humane Society of the United States

For a publications catalog, send a stamped, self-addressed envelope to

> The Humane Society of the United States
> 2100 L Street, NW
> Washington, DC 20037
> 202-452-1100

Or visit the HSUS Web site at

> http://www.hsus.org/

International Veterinary Acupuncture Society

For a list of veterinary acupuncturists in your area, send a stamped, self-addressed envelope to

> IVAS
> David H. Jaggar
> P.O. Box 2174
> Nederland, CO 80466-2024

LISTSERV

Feline-L

FELINE-L is a discussion list for and about all kinds of cats. Postings range from care and feeding of your household tom or tabby to scientific research concerning any aspect of wild or domestic feline populations. To subscribe to FELINE-L, send email to

> <LISTSERV@PSUVM.BITNET> (Bitnet users)

> <LISTSERV@PSUVM.PSU.EDU> (Internet users)

Include a blank subject line and the following command as the first (and only) line of the message body:

> SUBSCRIBE FELINE-L *Your Full Name*

OTHER WORLD WIDE WEB SITES OF INTEREST

American Veterinary Medical Association

http://www.avma.org/home.html

Check out its pet information page called Care for Pets at

http://www.avma.org/care4pets/

Breeder Lists
Visit these Web sites for directories of breeders:

http://www.fanciers.com/
http://www.breedlist.com

Cornell Feline Health Center
Visit this Web site of the famous Feline Health Center for information on a variety of cat-care topics:

http://web.vet.cornell.edu/public/fhc/FelineHealth.html

Cyber-Pet
Visit this great commercial Web site that's informative and fun:

http://www.cyberpet.com/

Dr. Jim's Animal Clinic for Cats and Dogs
Famous veterinarian, radio and television personality and author of *Dr. Jim's Animal Clinic for Cats* offers pet lovers advice on health, behavior and general cat-care topics. Visit his Web site at

http://www.dvmedia.com/vetclinic.html

Commercial Sites
Check out these commercial sites that offer lots of pet-care information:

Purina™ Foods	http://www.purina.com/
Heinz Pet™ Foods	http://www.heinzpet.com/
Tidy Cat™ Litter	http://www.tidycat.com/

RECOMMENDED READING

Magazines

The major cat magazines include *Cat Fancy*, *CATS* and *I Love Cats*. They are available at most newsstands.

Books

Behavior

Ackerman, Lowell, D.V.M., et al. *Cat Behavior and Training: Veterinary Advice for Cat Owners*. Neptune, NJ: TFH Publications, 1996.

Caras, Roger A. *A Cat is Watching: a Look at the Way Cats See Us*. New York: Simon & Schuster, 1989.

Dodman, Nicholas, Ph.D. *The Cat Who Cried for Help: Attitudes, Emotions and the Psychology of Cats*. New York: Bantam, 1997.

Eckstein, Warren, and Fay Eckstein. *How to Get Your Cat to do What You Want*. New York: Villard Books, 1990.

Padwee, Howard, Ph.D. *The Cat Who Couldn't See in the Dark: Veterinary Mysteries and Advice on Feline Care and Behavior*. Chapters Publishing, 1997.

Tabor, Roger, *Understanding Cats: Their History, Nature and Behavior*. Reader's Digest Books, 1997.

Wright, John C., Ph.D. and Judi Wright Lashnits. *Is Your Cat Crazy? Solutions from the Casebook of a Cat Therapist*. New York: Macmillan Publishing, 1994.

General Cat Care

Commings, Karen. *The Shorthaired Cat: An Owner's Guide to a Happy, Healthy Pet*. New York: Howell Book House, 1996.

Fogle, Bruce, D.V.M. *101 Questions Your Cat Would Ask Its Vet if Your Cat Could Talk*. New York: Carroll & Graf Publishers, Inc., 1993.

Fox, Michael W., Ph.D. *Super Cat*. New York: Howell Book House, 1990.

Humphries, Jim, D.V.M. *Dr. Jim's Animal Clinic for Cats: What People Want to Know*. New York: Howell Book House, 1994.

Sadler, Amy. *The Longhaired Cat: An Owner's Guide to a Happy, Healthy Pet*. New York: Howell Book House, 1996.

Shojai, Amy. *Kitten Care and Training: An Owner's Guide to a Happy, Healthy Pet*. New York: Howell Book House, 1996.

Health Care

Carlson, Delbert G., D.V.M. and James M. Giffin, M.D., *Cat Owner's Home Veterinary Handbook*. New York: Howell Book House, 1995.

The Doctors' Book of Home Remedies for Dogs and Cats. Emmaus, PA: Rodale Press, 1996.

Frazier, Anitra with Norma Eckroate. *The New Natural Cat*. New York: Plume, 1990.

Mammato, Bobbie, D.V.M., *First Aid for Pets*, American Red Cross and Humans Society of the United States.

McGinnis, Terri, D.V.M. *The Well Cat Book: The Classic Comprehensive Handbook of Cat Care*. New York: Random House, 1993.

Muller, Ulrike and H. Alfred Muller, *Healthy Cat, Happy Cat: A Complete Guide to Cat Diseases and their Treatments*. Hauppauge, New York: Barron's Educational Series, Inc., 1995.

Pitcairn, Richard H., D.V.M., Ph.D., and Susan Hubble Pitcairn. *Dr. Pitcairn's Complete Guide to Natural Health for Dogs and Cats*. Emmaus, PA: Rodale Press, 1982.

Schwartz, Cheryl, D.V.M. *Four Paws, Five Directions: A Guide to Chinese Medicine for Cats and Dogs*. Berkeley, CA: Celestial Arts, 1996.

Siegal, Mordecai, ed., *The Cornell Book of the Cat*, rev. 2nd edition. New York: Random House, 1997.

Thornton, Kim Campbell and John Hamil, D.V.M. *Your Aging Cat*. New York: Howell Book House, 1997.

Just for Fun

Gonzales, Philip. *The Dog Who Rescues Cats: the True Story of Ginney*. New York: HarperCollins Publishers, 1996.

Heim, Judy. *Internet for Cats: a Guide to How You and Your Cat can Prowl the Information Superhighway Together*. Daly City, CA: No Starch Press, 1996.

Walters, Heather MacLean. *Take Your Pet Along: 1001 Places to Stay with Your Pet*. Chester, NJ: M.C.E., 1995.

Index

(Note: The titles of shelter programs and newsletters are italicized.)

A